28 Days
— to —
Powerful
Prayer

28 Days
—to—
Powerful
Prayer

DAVE EARLEY

BARBOUR BOOKS
An Imprint of Barbour Publishing, Inc.

Contents

Introduction: Teach Us to Pray 7

Part I: The Plan, Privilege, and Power of Prayer
Day 1: Starting Your Prayer Adventure 9
Day 2: My Prayer Plan. 15
Day 3: Accessing God's Throne. 20
Day 4: Connecting with Your Heavenly Father 26
Day 5: Asking and Receiving 31
Day 6: Changing History 37
Day 7: Replacing Anxiety with Peace. 43

Part II: The Daily Prayers
Day 8: The Prayer of Thanksgiving 48
Day 9: The Prayer of Praise 55
Day 10: The Prayer of Confession and Heart Cleansing 62
Day 11: The Prayer of Supplication 69
Day 12: The Prayer of Intercession 75
Day 13: The Prayer of Surrender 81
Day 14: The Prayer of Liberation. 88

Part III: Prayer Boosters
Day 15: Removing Roadblocks to Answered Prayer 95
Day 16: Humility in Prayer 102
Day 17: Persistence in Prayer. 109
Day 18: Faith in Prayer 116
Day 19: Unity in Prayer 122
Day 20: Resolution in Prayer 129
Day 21: When Prayer Goes Unanswered 135

Part IV: Prayer Issues
Day 22: Prayer That Sparks War in the Heavens. 143
Day 23: Praying for Spiritual Leaders. 149
Day 24: Praying with Paul for Others 156

Day 25: Praying the Scriptures 162
Day 26: Prayer and Fasting 168
Day 27: Praying in a Spiritual Desert 174
Day 28: Praying When You Need a Miracle. 180

Final Thoughts 187
Suggestions for Using This Book. 189

Introduction:
Teach Us to Pray

The disciples had been following Jesus closely for about a year. They were amazed at how He spoke with such authority, at the compassion He showed the hurting, and at His miraculous power. They were impressed with how He could command the attention of huge crowds yet minister just as skillfully in a one-on-one setting.

People brought Jesus a steady stream of difficult questions, overwhelming dilemmas, and staggering burdens. Yet He almost effortlessly flowed through each encounter with astounding grace, poise, and power.

What was Jesus' secret? Where did He get His stunning inner strength and amazing wisdom?

It's as simple as this: Jesus was an incredible person of prayer. His prayers are referenced twenty-seven times in scripture. As we read the Gospels, we consistently see Jesus praying in all sorts of situations and settings:

- He prayed in the morning and in the evening (Mark 1:35; Matthew 14:23).
- He prayed all night (Luke 6:12).
- He prayed often (Luke 5:16).
- He prayed at His baptism (Luke 3:21).
- He prayed on a mountain (Matthew 6:36; 14:23), in the wilderness (Luke 5:16), and in the Garden of Gethsemane prior to His crucifixion (Matthew 26:36–44).
- He prayed alone (Mark 1:35; Luke 9:18).
- He prayed for children (Matthew 19:13).
- He prayed for His disciples and for their disciples (Luke 22:35; John 17:1–25).
- He prayed for Himself (Matthew 26:39; Mark 14:35).
- He prays for you today in heaven (Romans 8:34; Hebrews 7:25).

After following and observing Jesus, the disciples could see what made Him such an incredible teacher and miracle-worker. They knew that it all flowed from His powerful prayer life. So, when they had an opportunity to ask Him anything they wanted, they made this simple request:

"Lord, teach us to pray."
Luke 11:1

As we begin our twenty-eight days to powerful prayer, that should be our prayer as well: *Lord, teach us to pray.*

The goal of this book is to lead you on your own prayer adventure to deepen and strengthen your relationship with God. If you apply what you read, your prayer life will be wonderfully expanded and renewed as you learn to approach God in fresh ways. This twenty-eight-day prayer journey is an adventure that will change your life!

I suggest that you read a chapter each day for a month and then pray using what you've learned. It has been said that it takes two to three weeks to develop a new habit and four weeks to become comfortable with it. Twenty-eight days is the ideal length to help you develop a lasting habit of strong, powerful prayer.

As you launch into this prayer journey, why don't you start now by bowing your head and inviting the Holy Spirit to teach you to pray?

That's a prayer request He's delighted to grant you today.

THE PLAN, PRIVILEGE, AND POWER OF PRAYER

Starting Your Prayer Adventure

Do you want a deeper relationship with your heavenly Father? Would you like to be closer to His heart? Do you hunger to feel as though you really are on a first-name basis with the Creator of this vast universe?

You can.

Would you like 24-7 access to God's help during your neediest moments? While you are at it, how would you like to be done with worry? Wouldn't it be nice to have peace that fills your heart and mind in even the toughest circumstances?

It is possible.

Could I interest you in having divine wisdom into the thorniest spiritual matters? Would you like to be the recipient of God's best gifts and greatest blessings? How would you feel about adding divine power to your service? Would greater insight into biblical truth interest you?

It is all available, and much more.

You really can have all these great benefits plus many others. There is just one primary prerequisite: you must become a person of prayer.

And you can.

The Bible promises it, many of its characters model it, and countless others have experienced it. You can too. I'll help. If you put in the time, effort, and energy, I'll give you a proven plan that works.

This twenty-eight-day adventure with powerful prayer is

for you. But before we get into that, let me tell you about a big adventure I enjoyed when I was just a kid.

An Ice Cream Odyssey

When I was nine years old, my dad drove me to the downtown section of our small town. We parked in front of a crumbling brick building and got out of the car. I was nervous because Dad had told me I was on my way to my first job interview. I shyly followed him into a large, cold room furnished with only a battered army-green metal desk and a worn wooden swivel chair. In the chair sat a bald, round man, happily chewing on his cigar.

My father walked me up to the desk and introduced me to the man who would be my new boss, Mr. Fee, who was in charge of local delivery for the Columbus Dispatch Printing Company. Behind him was a sign that said DELIVERY BOYS MUST BE AT LEAST 12 YEARS OLD.

Mr. Fee looked me over and shook his head. "He looks pretty small to me," he observed. "Are you sure he can handle it?"

"He can handle it," Dad said. "I'll help him."

Thus began my career as a paperboy. For the next eight years, I delivered newspapers.

There were things I did not like about being a paperboy. Big barking dogs scared me. People who never seemed to be able to come up with the money to pay their bill frustrated me. And delivering newspapers in the rain was never fun.

But there was one thing I immediately liked about my job. I discovered that after I delivered my last paper, my route home took me past the local Baskin-Robbins ice cream shop. There I would purchase a strawberry ice cream cone.

The first few days of strawberry ice cream cones were wonderful. . .but then disaster struck. As usual, after I had delivered my last paper, I popped in the door of Baskin-Robbins. This time, however, when the man behind the counter saw me, he sadly shook his head. "Sorry, kid," he said. "We ran out of strawberry and won't get any more for a while."

It must have looked to him like I was going to cry, be
he quickly added, "But don't worry. We have thirty more fl
Have you ever tried butter pecan?"

I shook my head skeptically.

He reached down and scooped out a huge cone of butter
pecan. I hesitantly took a lick of the honey-colored ice cream
with soft brown nuts and smiled. It was so smooth and creamy.

The next day, I tested watermelon ice. It was refreshingly
tart, yet sweet.

Then I tried blackberry. It was a lot like strawberry, except it
had more of a kick.

Day after day for the next week, I eagerly anticipated the
next flavor in my ice cream odyssey. They had thirty-one flavors!
I could not believe my good fortune.

But when I was on flavor number eight in my joyous journey,
it all came to a sad and sudden halt. I had run out of money. I
would not be paid for several more weeks, and my dad did not
loan money, especially for ice cream.[1]

A Prayer Adventure

Years after my ice cream adventure, when I was in high school, I
surrendered my life to Jesus. Not long after that, I led worship at
a retreat for the high school youth group at my friend's church.
The lady who spoke to us that weekend talked about prayer. In
one of her sessions, she gave us a handout describing five aspects of prayer: thanksgiving, praise, confession, supplication,
and intercession. Her teaching exploded my understanding of
prayer and set me on a prayer adventure that far surpassed my
ice cream odyssey.

Ice cream is a glorious treat, but prayer is infinitely more
glorious than ice cream could ever be, simply because prayer
connects us with our heavenly Father. He is wondrously good,
infinitely powerful, and comfortingly wise. He is and has all we
need. And He gives us access to Himself through prayer.

But ice cream and prayer are alike in that both come in many

..avors. Prayer can have many aspects, and the various elements of prayer can overlap and flow into each other. Like ice cream, these elements may taste better mixed with one another. Just as many people like chocolate and peanut butter mixed together, you may like to mix two or more "flavors" of prayer in one session. For example, one morning I enjoyed an hour in prayer and used six different aspects of prayer—thanksgiving, praise, confession, surrender, supplication, and intercession.

Even though most people like several flavors of ice cream, they have a flavor they like more than the others. Likewise, you will use some elements of prayer more often than others. You may find yourself using some aspects every day. Some fit specific seasons and situations of life better than others. You will see this as you apply and enjoy them.

Your Twenty-Eight Days to Powerful Prayer

Maybe you've never thought of it this way, but your life of prayer truly can be a life-changing adventure. As you continue on through Day 28 of this book, you'll find that you can have a broader, deeper prayer life that will draw you closer to God's heart than you've ever been before. You'll see the wonderful ways in which you can have God's ear so that you can thank Him for all He's done for you, praise Him for who He is, go to Him to confess your sins, give yourself completely to Him, bring Him your requests, and pray for those He's placed in your life.

Suggestions for More Effective Prayer

Now let's look at some practical, simple steps you can take to help you build a strong foundation for a deeper prayer life. Each of these five steps can help you build a more powerful prayer life during the next twenty-seven days, and they each include a space where you can jot down your own personalized plan:

1. *Choose a time to pray.* Set aside time each day to read a chapter of this book and pray. It could be first thing in the morning or

during your lunch hour, or it could be the last thing you do at night. The right time is the time that works best for you.

My primary time to pray will be:

2. Determine an amount of time for prayer. We all have 24 hours, or 1,440 minutes, in a day. Giving God 15, or 30, or 60 minutes each day for study and prayer can be a life-changing experience. Select an amount of time daily for prayer. After the first month, you will find that you have grown significantly in your prayer life.

My usual amount of time in prayer will be:

3. Select a primary place for prayer. Moses used a tent and Jesus liked to pray outside. Your place for prayer could be at a desk, at the kitchen table, on a walk, in your car, or on your bed.

My primary place of prayer will be:

4. Ask a friend to pray with you. Jesus promised added insight and answers when two or more agree in prayer (Matthew 18:19). My wife, Cathy, and I try to pray together at ten every night. When my kids were teenagers, we prayed together as a family four nights a week. My friends Connie and Marilyn are widows, and they pray together over the phone every afternoon. Ask a friend to read this book along with you. Get together a few times a week to share what you have learned and to pray together, either in person or over the phone.

The person(s) I will ask to be my prayer partner(s) will be:

5. Read a chapter of this book and pray. Each chapter (or day) of this book covers different truths about prayer. After reading a chapter, answer the questions at the end, then apply the practical suggestions given to aid your journey to more powerful prayer.

My goal is to read _____ chapters of this book a week.

Questions to Consider

1. What excites you about beginning this twenty-eight-day adventure in powerful prayer?
2. What time each day do you plan to read this book and pray?
3. How much time will you set aside for reading and prayer each day?
4. Where do you plan to read this book and pray each day?
5. Which of your friends could you ask to join you in your prayer journey?

Notes

1. I adapted this story from one of my books that is no longer in print.

THE PLAN, PRIVILEGE, AND POWER OF PRAYER

My Prayer Plan

One day when I was eighteen years old, I was sitting in a church service listening to an inspiring speaker talk about the importance of prayer. He was preaching on the passage in which Jesus wrestled with the Father in prayer on the night He was arrested, then returned to His disciples, who were sound asleep. "Couldn't you men keep watch with me for *one hour*?" He asked Peter (Matthew 26:40 emphasis added).

The speaker talked about the importance of devoting time to prayer and about some amazing answers to prayer God had given him. He also talked about how his life wonderfully changed when he committed himself to praying an hour a day.

As this man concluded his talk, he challenged us to stand up if we were willing to make a commitment to pray one full hour each day. I stood, my heart pounding and my mind racing with the possibilities of having a more powerful prayer life.

I did not fully realize it then, but that was one of the best decisions I've ever made. The best way to learn to pray, after all, is by praying.

Building My Prayer Life

The college I attended was brand new and did not even have dorms when I was a freshman. I lived with a handful of other young men in the top of an old hospital building in the ghetto. There were four of us to a dorm room, and eight of us shared a bathroom. There were no closets and little privacy.

The best thing about that hospital/makeshift dorm was the operating room. It was on the top floor and had a lot of windows to let in light. It overlooked the street below, aptly named Grace Street. The only furniture in the room was a cold gray metal desk and a stiff metal chair.

My life changed in that operating room.

The day after I made my commitment to pray for an hour a day, I went to the operating room at my appointed time and sat down at the desk and began to pray. After a while I could not think of much else to pray about, so I stopped and looked at my watch. Only ten minutes had gone by. I had stood in front of all those people and said I would pray an hour a day. What would I do for the next fifty minutes?

Over the next few days, I dug into notes I had taken and handouts I had been given about prayer since I had become a Christian. I cobbled together a plan for prayer that I have followed in one way or another ever since. That plan became my foundation for building a powerful prayer life.

My Plan for Daily Prayer

The plan I developed was simple and balanced. It involved several aspects of prayer that I'll cover in more detail later in this book. It consisted of two primary steps: (1) letting God speak to me through His Word, and (2) speaking to God in prayer.

Here's how it worked for me:

1. *Listening to God.* When I constructed my plan, I figured it was best to let God speak to me through His written Word before I talked to Him in prayer. That's why I started every day by praying this scripture verse: *Open my eyes that I may see wonderful things in your law* (Psalm 119:18).

After that short prayer, I took the following steps as I read from the Bible:

Read: I read one psalm each day.

Key verse: I wrote down the words of a key verse from that psalm.

Study: I wrote down three sentences answering the three primary questions of Bible study:

- What does it say?
- What does it mean?
- How can I apply it to my life?

Prayer application: Next, I wrote down several aspects of prayer that came from the psalm I had just read:

- Praise God because He is:
- I thank God because He does:
- I confess to God that I have:
- I ask God to:

It amazed me how the words of the psalm of the day almost always had pertinent application for my life. As I prayed through the psalms in that operating room, the Holy Spirit used the scalpel of His Word to operate on my heart, cutting out fear, doubt, intimidation, loneliness, confusion, and bitterness.

When I had finished my Bible reading, I moved on to my next step.

2. *Talking to God in prayer.* I structured my talks with God loosely around the five aspects of prayer that I had learned about after I got saved: thanksgiving, praise, confession, supplication, and intercession. I stood up and walked around the room and prayed, spending a few minutes on each one:

Thanksgiving: This means expressing gratitude to God for what He has done. I reflected on the previous day, thinking of all the things for which I could be thankful. I also gave thanks for the bigger blessings of the previous few weeks or months. (See more on Thanksgiving in Day 8.)

Praise: Praise is worshipping God for who He is. I was learning more and more about God, so I would praise Him for things about Him that are true of the Lord and no one else. For example, He alone is infinite, all-knowing, all-powerful, everywhere present, perfect, and holy. (See more on Praise in Day 9.)

I also praised Him by His names and titles in the Bible (Savior, Redeemer, Creator, King of Kings, Father, Wonderful Counselor, the Way, the Truth, and the Life.)

Confession: When we engage in confession, we are agreeing with God about our sin. When I prayed, I asked the Holy Spirit to point out any aspect of my life that displeased Him. I would review the previous twenty-four hours and address the things I had done, the words I had said, and the things I had thought. (See more on Confession in Day 10.)

Supplication: Supplication is asking God to provide for your needs. I had very little money at this time in my life. Anything I wanted beyond room and board had to come to me as an answer to prayer. I also needed wisdom for my classes. I was also on the wrestling team and needed help in my competitions. Beyond that, I needed wisdom because I worked with middle school students at my church. (See more on Supplication in Day 11.)

Intercession: Intercession is standing in the gap and praying for others. (See more on Intercession in Day 12.) As part of my plan, I prayed every day for:

every day
- My family members to be saved
- My roommates
- The middle school kids I worked with at church

I also focused my prayers on one special area each day of the week:

weekly
- Monday: friends from high school
- Tuesday: the lost
- Wednesday: my pastor
- Thursday: government leaders
- Friday: missionaries and church planters
- Saturday and Sunday: my church and its upcoming worship services

At first, using my prayer plan was rather awkward. I struggled to fill up a whole hour in prayer. But within a week or two, the plan gave me the structure I needed to begin to go places in prayer that I did not know were possible. As I stuck with my plan, I found that the hour of prayer began to fly by. Eventually, I had to make myself stop at an hour because I had to get on to my schoolwork.

Your Twenty-Eight Days to Powerful Prayer

Maybe my plan seems overwhelming to you. Maybe praying for a whole hour each day seems like an impossibility. The goal, however, is to make a commitment to your prayer life and to be consistent.

You don't need to adopt my plan. As you read through this book, you can develop *your own plan*. Just start small and add to it. As you work through this book, you will grow in your prayer life and begin to add the pieces and parts you need each day. You will also gain understanding of aspects of prayer you might add in the future. I've written this book not merely to give you inspiring information about prayer but also to encourage you to *apply* that information as you build your own powerful life of prayer. Please take a few minutes and write down your own plan for prayer:

Questions to Consider

1. What part of this chapter most inspired or interested you?
2. Do you have a plan for your prayer life? If so, what is your plan?
3. What aspects of prayer mentioned in this chapter would you like to add to your daily prayer plan?
4. How long are you going to set aside for prayer each day?
5. Where is the place you plan on praying each day?

DAY 3

THE PLAN, PRIVILEGE, AND POWER OF PRAYER

Accessing God's Throne

Do you tend to view prayer more as a mystery, a duty, a spiritual discipline, or a privilege?

Do you feel as though access to God's presence is limited to the spiritually elite?

Is it right to think that you can talk to God anytime about anything?

If a seven-year-old asked you what prayer is, how would you answer?

Let's consider these questions as we make our way through today's chapter.

What Is Prayer?

The Bible has much to say about the true nature of prayer. Here are five truths about prayer taken directly from God's Word:

1. Prayer is an amazing privilege. When Jesus lived on earth, the center of Jewish religious life was the temple in Jerusalem. That was where priests offered sacrifices and worshipped every day (1 Chronicles 16:37–42).

In the time of Jesus, the temple was divided into these main areas:

- the court of the Gentiles (where anyone could enter)
- the court of women (reserved for ritually pure Jewish women)

- the court of the Israelites (reserved for ritually pure Jewish men)
- the temple court where sacrifices were made
- the Holy Place (reserved for priests)
- the innermost chamber, also called the Holy of Holies

A huge, thick, beautiful curtain separated the Holy of Holies from the rest of the temple. Behind the veil was the altar and the ark of the covenant, which was the earthly residence of God's presence and glory (Hebrews 9:1–9). The curtain signified the fact that man was separated from God by sin (Isaiah 59:1–2). Only the high priest could enter the Holy of Holies and then only once a year, on the Day of Atonement, to offer a sacrifice for the sins of the nation (Leviticus 16; Hebrews 9:7; Exodus 30:10).

Think about that. Only one man could come into God's presence—and on only one day a year. Access to the presence of God was severely limited to the one member of the highly privileged elite and then only on very rare occasions.

But Jesus changed all that!

When Jesus was crucified, *He* became the permanent offering for sin (Isaiah 53:5). The moment He died, the curtain in the temple was split from top to bottom (Matthew 27:45–51). This was no small thing. The massive curtain was sixty feet high and three to four inches thick.

The splitting of the curtain graphically signified that Jesus' sacrifice on the Cross was sufficient atonement for the sins of the world. Neither the daily sacrifices for sins nor the annual sacrifices were necessary any longer.

The splitting of the curtain also signified that access to God was no longer limited. Every child of God now has access to His throne. As Jesus' body was torn for us, the curtain was torn in two, giving us open access to God (Hebrews 10:19–22). We now have an open invitation to "approach God's throne of grace with confidence, so that we may receive mercy and find grace to help us in our time of need" (Hebrews 4:16). God welcomes us to come to Him, and He promises to listen to us: "This is the confidence we have in approaching God: that if we ask anything according to his will, he hears us" (1 John 5:14).

What a privilege!

From the moment Jesus died on the Cross for us and the curtain was torn, all of God's children have had open access to His throne of grace. Unlike the high priest, we can come every day, at any time, and as often as we like. Unlike the high priest, we do not have to offer sacrifice for sin, because Jesus is our once-for-all-time sacrifice. We now have a standing invitation to come to God and ask for help and for the things we need.

This is astounding!

Prayer is taking advantage of the great privilege of access to God He has granted. It is viewing our daily time with the Lord as boldly and confidently entering the Holy of Holies to speak with Him.

2. Prayer is talking with God. Moses understood that prayer is simply talking with his God. He set up a tent (called the tent of meeting) where he could go daily to meet with God. Here he carried on simple, honest, daily dialogue with God. Instead of being offended at Moses' often frank familiarity, "The LORD would speak to Moses face to face, as one speaks to a friend" (Exodus 33:11).

If you want to build a strong prayer life, keep it simple. You do not need to approach God with lofty words or eloquent phrases. He is not impressed with melodramatic or theatrical intonations. Be real. Be authentic. Open your heart and your mouth and talk with God as you would with a friend.

3. Prayer can be an ongoing conversation with God. The apostle Paul told the Thessalonian church to "pray continually" (1 Thessalonians 5:17). This does not mean we should spend twenty-four hours a day on our knees with our eyes closed and our hands clasped tightly in front of us. It means that prayer is to be an ongoing conversation with God. It means we can say little prayers here and there throughout the day.

Prayer is talking to God about the daily aspects of life. It is telling the Father about our thoughts, dreams, hurts, sorrows, joys, and questions. It is turning all our ordinary events and experiences into prayer.

4. Prayer is practicing the presence of God. As a young Christian, I read a book called *The Practice of the Presence of God.*[1] It was written by a large, clumsy man named Nicholas, who was later known as Brother Lawrence. Nicholas had the menial job of washing pots and pans in a large kitchen because he was considered too awkward to do anything else.

But Nicholas loved God deeply and set a goal of living in the Lord's presence all day long as he cleaned the pots and pans. He discovered that the way to sense God's presence all day was to have many conversations with Him throughout the day. Nicholas turned his kitchen into a personal holy of holies and tent of meeting. Because of the rich aura of God that began to perfume his presence, important people began to come from all around to seek the clumsy kitchen worker's advice on spiritual matters.

5. Prayer is like spiritual breathing. Prayer, like breathing, is essential for life. The great theologian and reformer Martin Luther called prayer the pulse of a Christian, saying, "A Christian without prayer is just as impossible as a living person without a pulse."[2]

One psalmist likened his need for God with the feeling of being spiritually thirsty and winded and cried out, "As the deer pants for streams of water, so my soul pants for you, my God" (Psalm 42:1). When you feel as though the pressures and problems of life are choking you, turn to prayer and take a drink. Pause and take a literal deep breath as you breathe out words of thanksgiving and praise to God.

Expressions of Prayer

God is infinite. We are needy. Because God has chosen to reveal Himself to us in many ways (Father, King, God, Shepherd, Friend,

Savior, Judge, Lover, Counselor, Guide, Physician) *and* because we have a variety of needs, effective prayer has various expressions. As you travel through this book, you will encounter a variety of aspects of prayer.

Prayer is:

- Accessing the throne of grace in time of need (Hebrews 4:16)
- Talking directly with God (Exodus 33:11)
- Enjoying an ongoing conversation with God (1 Thessalonians 5:16)
- Spiritual breathing (Psalm 42:1)
- Connecting with the Father's heart and crying, "Abba, Father" (Romans 8:15; Galatians 4:6)
- Positioning yourself to receive all the blessings God will give you (Matthew 7:7–11)
- Changing history (James 5:16–18)
- Actively replacing worry with peace (Philippians 4:6–7)
- Sparking spiritual war in the heavens (Daniel 10:1–12)
- Giving thanks to God for what He has done (1 Thessalonians 5:16–18)
- Declaring praise to God for who He is (Psalm 100)
- Cleansing your heart (Psalm 51)
- Asking God to meet your needs
- Asking God to meet the needs of others
- Surrendering everything that is a part of your life to God
- Choosing to forgive others
- Humbly crying out to God (Luke 18:13)
- Exercising faith (Matthew 21:21)
- Continuing to ask, seek, and knock (Luke 11:7–13)
- Trusting God even when the answers don't come
- Staying committed to God no matter what
- Continuing on when your heart is dry.
- Praying the scriptures
- Praying the prayers in the Bible for others

- Replacing food with prayer
- Claiming the promises of God

Your Twenty-Eight Days to Powerful Prayer

Yesterday we talked about establishing a time and place for daily prayer. Today we talked about praying to God throughout the day. A bird needs two wings to fly, and we, likewise, need our prayer to consist of two aspects: consistent daily time with God *and* talking with God all day.

Questions to Consider

1. What did you like or learn about the temple, the veil, and the holy of holies?
2. What appealed to you from the story of Nicholas?
3. From the "Prayer Is. . ." list, which three descriptions are most inspiring or interesting to you? Why?
4. If a seven-year-old asked you what prayer is, how would you answer after reading this chapter?
5. How can you apply what you have learned from this chapter to your prayer life today?

Notes

1. *The Practice of the Presence of God* (New Kensington, Pennsylvania: Whitaker House, 1982).
2. Martin Luther, quoted in Herman Wilhelm, *The Communion of the Christian with God; Described on the Basis of Luther's Statements* (London: Hard Press Publishing, 1906), 322.

THE PLAN, PRIVILEGE, AND POWER OF PRAYER

Connecting with Your Heavenly Father

The young man was exhausted and hungry, and he smelled like a pig. Nothing was going right for him. He had lost his money, his friends, his dignity, and his hope.

He had been away from home a long time. . .too long. *Home.* That word conjured so many good memories. Big meals around the table. His own room. Good steady work and generous pay. And Father. The one thing he missed most of all was Father.

He could hear his father's voice in his head. It was deep and rich, yet warm. It could give him joy and hope like no one else's voice. Father did not say many words, but they were always true and wise, and, when appropriate, they could cut through to the core of the issue. But, best of all, Father's voice was always full of love, even on the day the young man left.

Give me my share. Why did he have to say that to his father that day? He could tell that his arrogant departure speech had hurt Father deeply. How he would love to take back every stupid word. But it was too late for that. He had made a fool of himself, had wasted his inheritance, and, worst of all, had hurt Father.

The best he could do now was to go back and say, "Father, I have sinned against heaven and against you. I am no longer worthy to be called your son; make me like one of your hired servants" (Luke 15:18–19).

Out of options, the young man headed back to his father's house. But before he even made it all the way back home, the most amazing thing happened:

While he was still a long way off, his father saw him and was filled with compassion for him; he ran to his son, threw his arms around him and kissed him.
LUKE 15:20

Jesus told us this story of the prodigal son (Luke 15:32) to show us the Father-heart of God. It is one of my favorite stories, and it reveals one of the foundational aspects of prayer: nothing connects us with our heavenly Father like prayer.

Our Father...

When Jesus' disciples asked Him to teach them to pray, He gave them a model prayer to follow (Luke 11:2–4). The prayer begins with words that teach us the core of prayer: "Our Father." Prayer is not impressing, flattering, cajoling, or begging God. Prayer is simply talking with your Father in heaven:

- Prayer is speaking with your heavenly Father personally: *Our Father in heaven*
- Prayer is speaking with your heavenly Father reverently: *Hallowed be Your name*
- Prayer is speaking with your heavenly Father purposely: *Your kingdom come*
- Prayer is speaking with your heavenly Father submissively: *Your will be done*
- Prayer is speaking with your heavenly Father dependently: *Give us day by day our daily bread*

Prayer to your heavenly Father isn't that complicated or difficult. In fact, it is easy when you realize that He:

- really loves you: "See what great love the Father has lavished on us, that we should be called children of God!" (1 John 3:1).
- deeply cares for you: "As a father has compassion on his children, so the LORD has compassion on those who fear him" (Psalm 103:13).

- is very near when you are hurting: "The LORD is close to the brokenhearted and saves those who are crushed in spirit" (Psalm 34:18).

"Abba, Father"

On the night of the Last Supper, Jesus knew that the shadow of the Cross loomed over Him. In the Garden of Gethsemane, He agonized about the horrors that were coming. As was His practice, Jesus turned every problem into prayer. In His anguish, He uttered a prayer of previously unseen intensity and intimacy:

> "Abba, Father," he said, "everything is possible for you. Take this cup from me. Yet not what I will, but what you will."
> MARK 14:36

The word *Abba* is an Aramaic term. First-century Jews spoke Hebrew at the temple and in school. They spoke Greek in the marketplace, but they spoke Aramaic at home and with the family. *Abba* is the most intimate term available in Hebrew, Greek, or Aramaic to express a child's tender relationship with his father, and as such only children used the word. It could be translated as "Father" or "Daddy" or "Papa."

The term *Abba* describes the unique relationship Jesus shared with His heavenly Father. But what is astounding is that we can enjoy the same privilege of intimacy with the Father that Jesus the Son shared with the Father when He walked on the earth.

The apostle Paul used the word *Abba* when he wrote about the amazing access God has granted to believers under the New Covenant:

> The Spirit you received does not make you slaves, so that you live in fear again; rather, the Spirit you received brought about your adoption to sonship. And by him we cry, "Abba, Father." The Spirit himself testifies with our spirit that we are God's children.
> ROMANS 8:15–16

> *Because you are his sons, God sent the Spirit of his Son into our hearts, the Spirit who calls out, "Abba, Father." So you are no longer a slave, but God's child; and since you are his child, God has made you also an heir.*
> GALATIANS 4:6–7

Through redemption and salvation, we are no longer God's enemies, and He has not made us His slaves or servants. Much better, we become His sons and daughters. We come to God as our *Abba* as we enjoy intimate access to Him and to our inheritance in Christ.

Abba prayer is the special privilege of the New Testament saint. In the Old Testament, believers were not allowed such personal access to God. They certainly were not encouraged to call Him "Father," let alone "Daddy." According to Professor Joachim Jeremias, "There is not a single example of the use of *abba* in the whole of Jewish literature."[1]

Sadly, many Christians today are afraid to pray out loud. It is as though they are afraid of making a mistake or not doing it right. We can overcome that fear when we understand that prayer, at its heart, is simply talking with our heavenly Father (Matthew 6:9). A child does not need special words to talk with his daddy. All he needs to do is take his hand or crawl into his lap and talk. Because his daddy loves him, he is happy to listen to him jabber away about anything on his mind.

So it is with our heavenly Father when we come to Him to talk.

"Abba" Prayers

As a Christian, you can approach your heavenly Father with the *Abba* prayer of His beloved child. You have access to crawl into the Father's lap to receive His love, comfort, healing, and strength. Through *Abba* prayer, you can take our heavenly Daddy's hand when you fear for the future. You can cry out to *the* Father to be *your* Father and to "father" you through difficult seasons of life. You can bring your prodigal soul home to God and experience the Father running to you, throwing His arms around you, and giving you a hug and a kiss as He rejoices over your return.

Abba prayer expresses your ongoing and growing relationship with God. It is carrying on a never-ending conversation with your heavenly Father God about the daily stuff of life. It is chattering away to Daddy about all of our thoughts, events, hurts, sorrows, joys, and questions.

Your Twenty-Eight Days to Powerful Prayer

This week, as you address God in prayer, try using the terms *Abba* or *Dad* or *Daddy*. How does it feel? Practice talking to your heavenly Father through your day about everything in your day.

Questions

1. What were two things in this chapter that caught your attention? Why?
2. Do you feel confident that you have truly experienced the love of our heavenly Father? Why or why not?
3. Do you know what it is like to lose your little hand in Your heavenly Father's great big hand?
4. Are you now facing a situation you need your Father in heaven to "father" you through?
5. Have you ever heard *Abba*'s warm voice saying something like, "There, there, My child. It will be all right. Father is here. Let Daddy take care of it."

Notes

1. Joachim Jeremias, *The Prayers of Jesus* (Philadelphia: SCM, 1967), 11.

THE PLAN, PRIVILEGE, AND POWER OF PRAYER

Asking and Receiving

What do you need right now? Strength? Wisdom? Help? Favor? Blessing?

God's response to your need is simple: "Ask."

Prayer involves a variety of elements including listening, praising, confessing, forgiving, and surrendering. But in the Bible, prayer is primarily about asking and receiving things from God.

Good Gifts Come to Those Who Ask

Jesus once said this about asking your heavenly Father for things you need or want:

> *"Ask and it will be given to you; seek and you will find; knock and the door will be opened to you. For everyone who asks receives; the one who seeks finds; and to the one who knocks, the door will be opened. Which of you, if your son asks for bread, will give him a stone? Or if he asks for a fish, will give him a snake? If you, then, though you are evil, know how to give good gifts to your children, how much more will your Father in heaven give good gifts to those who ask him!"*
> MATTHEW 7:7–11

Jesus used the word *ask* five times in the above passage. He promised that those who ask will receive, those who seek will find, and those who knock will have the door opened to them.

He drove home the promise of God's generosity and goodness toward His children by pointing out that even imperfect, human fathers give their children good gifts. Our good Father in heaven, Jesus taught, can be depended upon all the more to give us good gifts when we ask Him.

In this passage, prayer can be understood as *asking and receiving good gifts from our Father in heaven*. Prayer is primarily asking. The words used most often for prayer in both the Old and New Testament have the primary meaning of asking.

How We Receive from God

God loves His children and loves to give us what we need. Many of His blessings are contingent on our prayers. He wants to give us good things, but we will not receive them unless we ask: "You do not have because you do not ask God" (James 4:2).

I believe that God has something like a special warehouse in heaven filled with special blessings He wants to do in us, for us, and through us. These blessings are labeled and on shelves waiting to be shipped. But He will never send these blessings unless we ask for them.

When I get to heaven, I hope I can go to that warehouse and see that every last blessing intended for me had been sent out. I would rather be guilty of asking for more than I receive than for receiving less than God wanted to give me.

"Don't Let It Rain"

Recently, our church planned an outdoor Easter community outreach event on one Saturday at 1 p.m. The problem was that all that week, the weather forecasts called for a 100 percent chance of heavy rain that Saturday. Several times that week, we met to pray, specifically asking God to stop the rain on Saturday.

It rained all day Thursday, and the early Friday forecasts predicted rain all day both Friday and Saturday. Rain poured down all day Friday and into the night. It was so loud that it woke many of us, so we continued praying individually for God to stop the rain.

When the sun came up Saturday morning, we found that God had answered our prayers. The rain had stopped, and not another drop fell all weekend. The event went off as planned and hundreds of people attended and heard about Jesus.

On Saturday evening, a local weather forecaster made an interesting observation. He said that even though it had rained all around our region on Saturday, there was "a donut of dryness" over our area. We believed that our heavenly Father had heard our prayers and given us the good gift of dryness we had asked for.

Obey the Command to Ask

When Jesus said, "Ask and it will be given to you" (Matthew 7:7), He was not offering a piece of advice or a suggestion. The word *ask* in this verse is an imperative verb, meaning it is a command He expected us to obey. Therefore, to have a need but fail to ask God to meet it is to disobey Jesus' clear command. If we are not asking, we are not obeying.

The Bible uses two Greek words for *ask*. One means to ask favor from an equal. The other means to make a request to a superior. Every time Jesus prayed to the Father, He used the word for asking a favor of an equal. Why? Because He was equal to the Father since He is God the Son.

On the other hand, every time Jesus commanded us to ask God for something, He used the word describing "making a request of a superior." Why? Because God is vastly superior to us. He knows things we do not know, has things we do not have, and is capable of things we cannot do.

Failing to pray and ask God for things shows spiritual independence and self-sufficiency. Jesus strongly condemned these attitudes when He rebuked the lukewarm Laodicean church (Revelation 3:14–17).

There is a popular, spiritual-sounding notion that asking in prayer is spiritual immaturity and listening is maturity. While there is some truth in that, we should be careful. We have only a few records of the content of Jesus' prayers. In all cases, Jesus did more in His prayer life than just listen. He also asked the Father for specific things.

If It Is Good to Have, It Is Good to Ask For

There should be no misunderstanding: God commands us to come to Him and ask for the things we need. But it should also be noted that our heavenly Father enjoys giving us more than what we need. He often gives us the things we deeply desire.

If it is good to have, it is good to ask for. It would be a sin to want something you could not legitimately ask God for, but if you deeply desire something that is not wrong for you to have, you should ask our heavenly Father for it.

I often pray like this:

Father, this desire does not seem to go away. I do not think it violates your Word. I believe that giving it to me would honor Your name and give You greater glory. If it is wrong for me to have or if it is something You do not want me to have, please take the desire away. But if it is good for me to have and if You want to give it to me, then please do so.

For several years, I had a desire to become a published author. I didn't *need* to be published in order to survive or to provide for my family, but it was my strong desire.

After working hard to develop a book proposal, I sent it to several publishers. I was thrilled when the largest Christian book publisher in the world called and offered me a contract. However, I can look back at that time in my life and see that my motives were not pure. Through a bizarre set of circumstances, the book I wanted to author never became a reality. After that, I received a flurry of rejection letters.

God had said, "No!"

Still, the desire to positively impact people through my writing, which I knew God had given me, would not go away. In fact, it intensified. It burned so deeply inside of me that I begged God to either fulfill it or take it away.

At that time, I had been working with others to revamp the small group structure at my church. We had spent the previous few years training our leaders with some materials I had created.

After purifying my motives for being published, and after begging God to either fulfill my desire to write and publish or take the desire away, I came up with an idea to write a book for a small niche publisher that produced only books for small group leaders. I sent the company a proposal for a book titled *Eight Habits of Effective Small Group Leaders*. The company loved it and sent me a contract. I used the materials I had created for my church and turned them into a simple, practical, readable forty thousand-word book.

The book was released in 2001 and was sold solely through a small network and a website. I was pleasantly surprised when it exploded in popularity. In time it was translated into several languages, including Spanish, Portuguese, Korean, Japanese, and Chinese. To this day, it continues to sell thousands of copies each year and has opened doors for me to speak to large audiences and amazing churches all over the world.

Since then, God has allowed me to write and publish twenty-five books that have impacted hundreds of thousands of people. Eight are used as textbooks at Bible colleges and seminaries, and others have sold at Christian bookstores and in a variety of places, including airports and Walmart.

God gave me a good gift and the desire of my heart. He put the desire in me and fulfilled the desire through me. . .after I asked Him to.

Your Twenty-Eight Days to Powerful Prayer

God is our heavenly Father and He wants to bless us with good gifts. But sometimes He knows that what we think is a good gift is not actually the best thing for us. Prayer is not us dictating our will to God. Prayer is us cooperating with God to accomplish *His* will here on earth. That is why God answers prayers in one of three ways: "Yes," "No," or "Wait." Regardless of how God answers, He always does so out of love for us as our wise heavenly Father who knows what is best for us and for others.

Questions to Consider

1. What caught your attention as you read this chapter? Why?
2. Does it feel difficult for you to ask God for what you desire?
3. What is/are the burning desire(s) of your heart?
4. How do you feel about asking God to either fulfill these desires or remove them?

THE PLAN, PRIVILEGE, AND POWER OF PRAYER

Changing History

Does prayer really change things, or does it merely change us? Does prayer make a difference in real-life situations, or does it only give us comfort because it helps us open up about our needs and fears?

Have you ever asked yourself those questions? I have. Let me explain.

Prayer Changed History. . .and Me

When I was twenty-four years old, I was privileged to serve as the campus pastor of a large Christian college. I was in way over my head. I was underprepared, over-busy, understaffed, and thoroughly overwhelmed with the immensity of the responsibility. As a new husband, a full-time graduate student, and a full-time campus pastor, I went into Christmas break feeling drained, discouraged, exhausted, and empty. My faith was wavering.

To combat these feelings, I began three days of fasting and reading through the psalms. The third day, I read Psalm 106, which recounts how the Lord had blessed Israel as He delivered her from slavery in Egypt. The psalm describes how, despite their many blessings, the Israelites rebelled against the Lord. Eventually, God had had enough. He was ready to destroy the people of Israel and start over with a whole new group of people, people who would be the children and grandchildren of Moses.

Then I came to a verse that changed my life. The Lord used it to crush my doubts and restore my faith. It was as though the rest of the psalm were printed in black and white, but that one verse jumped out at me like it was written in neon lights:

> So he said he would destroy them—had not Moses, his chosen one, stood in the breach before him to keep his wrath from destroying them.
> Psalm 106:23

"*Had not Moses.*" Those three words in the middle of Psalm 106:23 spoke to my soul. Destruction would have come *had not Moses*. History would have been terribly altered *had not Moses*. Thousands would have died *had not Moses*.

Prayer had made a difference, a *big* difference. Prayer changed history!

It also changed me.

The Rest of the Story

At the college where I served, we were launching the new semester with four days of special services. We had scheduled a guest speaker to come in and lead us.

The student dorm leaders returned to campus a few days early to prepare for the semester. When I spoke to them, I shared my faith struggle and Moses' prayer in Psalm 106:23. I challenged them to pray for the struggling students in their dorms as Moses had prayed for his nation.

They did. Many of them led all-night prayer meetings in their dorms.

Over the next few days, the rest of the students arrived. On Sunday night, I picked up the guest speaker and drove him to the first service of the special meetings.

I was concerned because I didn't think he was spiritually ready to lead us into a new semester. But it did not matter. God showed up powerfully that night. Dozens and dozens of students got right with God, not in response to the guest speaker's preaching, but as a result of the prayers of their dorm leaders.

Prayer had made a difference—a *big* difference.

Prayer Changed the Weather

During the time of the kings, Israel was reeling under the ungodly leadership of wicked King Ahab and his even more evil wife, Jezebel. After assuming the throne, they began leading Israel deeply into idolatry by erecting altars and a temple to the false god Baal, the chief deity in that region. He was the demonic, thunderbolt god of rain and fertility. As an agrarian society, Israel relied on rain to grow its crops. This meant that pleasing Baal was essential, no matter the cost, even if it meant child sacrifice (Jeremiah 19:3–5).

God, however, had a praying man on the scene. Out of no-where, Elijah appeared and told Ahab that there would be no more rain until he said so (1 Kings 18:1).

Think about it: no rain! That was a big deal.

There was no rain for *three and a half years*, and then Elijah asked God to send rain again (1 Kings 18:42–45). Nothing could have been more crushing to Ahab's campaign of idolatry. Baal, the thunderbolt god of rain, would be shown as impotent before one man who knew how to pray.

Where did Elijah get the ability to withhold rain? His power to change the weather came from God, through prayer. The writer of the Book of James describes it like this:

> The heartfelt and persistent prayer of a righteous man (believer) can accomplish much [when put into action and made effective by God—it is dynamic and can have tremendous power]. Elijah was a man with a nature like ours [with the same physical, mental, and spiritual limitations and shortcomings], and he prayed intensely for it not to rain, and it did not rain on the earth for three years and six months. Then he prayed again, and the sky gave rain and the land produced its crops [as usual].
> James 5:16–18 AMP

I know what you are thinking: *Okay, Elijah changed the weather through prayer. But I'm not Elijah.*

God knew what you would think, so He made a point of adding the phrase, "Elijah was a man with a nature like ours" (James 5:17). In other words, Elijah was just as human as we are.

Again, I know what you are thinking: *But that was then, and this is now.*

Here's my answer: God has not changed! The Bible tells us so:

"I am the LORD, I do not change."
MALACHI 3:6 NKJV

Jesus Christ is the same yesterday and today and forever.
HEBREWS 13:8

The God of Elijah is still God. Prayer was powerful then, and it is still powerful now.

Just ask my mom.

The Rest of the Story

Several years ago, my wife, Cathy, was looking forward to a rather significant birthday. She always went out of her way to make our birthdays special. . .while I, in the midst of running three boys around and serving in a busy church, often forgot hers. We wanted to make this birthday very special, so I rented the local community pool and invited two hundred of Cathy's friends for a massive surprise pool party on the night before her birthday.

I got up the morning of the big day and checked the weather forecast. The weatherman excitedly pointed at the radar, which showed a massive storm moving across the state—directly toward our suburb. The storm was predicted to hit our area at exactly the time of the party.

I was worried. The pool was already booked every other night for the next month, and I learned that I could not get my money back, even if it rained. Also, this was in the days before cell phones and social media, so I had no way to quickly alert two hundred people not to come.

So I did what I often did when I didn't know what to do: I

called my mom.

My mother was a tiny lady, less than five feet tall and well under a hundred pounds. She did not really give her life to God until her late fifties. But after that, she lived the rest of her life on fire for Him. She had a very simple, childlike faith and a powerful prayer life.

I told her about the storm and asked, "Mom, what should I do?"

"Don't worry," she said.

"But what am I going to do?"

"I got this," she answered. "You go ahead and have the party."

The Rest of the Story, Part 2

Just after seven o'clock, after a nice dinner with a couple of friends, Cathy and I showed up at the pool "to pick up the kids," as I told her. Two hundred excited people jumped out and yelled, "Surprise!" and sang "Happy Birthday" to her. We had a great time. The sky was clear with not one drop of rain.

We got home and I turned on the eleven o'clock news. The lead story was about the massive storm that had hit central Ohio. The weatherman pointed at the screen behind him.

"As you can see," he said, "just a little before seven o'clock the storm was set to crash into Gahanna [our suburb]. Then the storm inexplicably split in two. It completely missed Gahanna and ended up causing minor flooding and a few power outages in Westerville and Reynoldsburg [the neighboring suburbs north and south of us]."

Then it hit me. One little lady who knew how to pray changed the weather. That was not three thousand years ago, and this was not a famous prophet. That was not even about the salvation of lost souls. That was for a birthday party.

Think about it. If God would do this for a birthday party, what will He do if you ask Him to help you win lost people to Jesus?

Only God knows how many prayers have changed the course of history. But you can know this: you can change history. . .from your knees.

Your Twenty–Eight Days to Powerful Prayer

Prayer changes things. List some areas in your life or your current situation where you would like God to make changes, and then use that list for prayer during these twenty-eight days.

1.
2.
3.
4.
5.
6.
7.

Questions to Consider

1. Which of the stories in this chapter did you like the best? Why?
2. Where do you need to see God making changes in your life?
3. What do you think it would take for you to develop the type of prayer life that can change history?
4. Will you accept the challenge to pray for a few big things you want to see God change?

THE PLAN, PRIVILEGE, AND POWER OF PRAYER

Replacing Anxiety with Peace

Do you often worry about the future?

Do thoughts of what *could* happen paralyze you?

Do you ever feel strangled by fear?

Do you feel torn between faith and anxiety?

Sometimes I do.

We are told that one out of five people in the United States struggles with severe anxiety.[1] But what should we Christians do when we feel overwhelmed by feelings of anxiety and depression?

I have learned the power of prayer to help me defeat anxiety. The apostle Paul was my teacher.

The Power of Prayer Over Anxiety

If I were Paul, I would probably have been anxious and depressed. He had been unjustly arrested, hauled far away to Rome, and thrown into prison by the maniacal emperor Nero. Alone and constantly chained to guards, he faced the possibility of execution every day. (In fact, a few years later, he *was* executed.)

Despite all this, Paul's letter to the church in Philippi, which he wrote while imprisoned in Rome, includes no mention of his own fear or anxiety. He does not whine or complain. He is filled with peace. He is not depressed or in despair. In fact, his letter to the Philippians has often been called "the Epistle of Joy."

How did Paul rise above his perilous situation?

Fortunately, he told us:

Do not be anxious about anything, but in every situation, by prayer and petition, with thanksgiving, present your requests to God. And the peace of God, which transcends all understanding, will guard your hearts and your minds in Christ Jesus.
PHILIPPIANS 4:6–7

Let's break down this passage.

1. Stop worrying: "Do not be anxious about anything," Paul wrote. The Greek word the apostle used for *anxious* speaks of being distracted, divided, and mentally defeated by the things over which we have little or no control. It speaks of being overwhelmed and filled with cares. It means to be pulled in opposite directions and divided into parts.

I know exactly what he means. On one hand, I want to respond to my problems with faith and confidence, but on the other, I am too easily filled with fear and concern. As a result, conflicting thoughts and emotions sometimes tear me apart.

The old English word for *worry* means "to strangle." I've been there also. It feels as though fear has its hands around my neck, strangling the peace, hope, and joy out of me.

Anxiety cuts off a sense of well-being and peace. It steals our focus and robs us of joy. Fear can quickly dominate our thinking. To make matters worse, the more we dwell on these negative thoughts, the stronger they become.

So Paul told his readers to stop being anxious.

But how?

2. Start praying: We have all tried not to worry only to grow more anxious. The only way to win over worry is to replace it with peace that comes as a result of grateful, comprehensive prayer: "but in every *situation*, by prayer and petition, with thanksgiving, present your requests to God" (Philippians 4:6).

In everything. Since the enemy loves to make anything and everything a reason to worry, we need to learn to make anything and everything a point of prayer. This means that no area of our lives, no situation we face or think we might face, is off limits when it comes to prayer.

By prayer. Paul's use of the word *prayer* in the above passage is to be understood in a broad sense as "prayer as an act of worship." Worship is a matter of looking to God and getting our eyes off everything other than Him. When we focus on our problems, they seem to grow. But when we focus on God, our problems shrink in comparison.

Consider Peter. When he kept his eyes on Jesus, he could walk on water. But when he focused on the waves and wind, he panicked and sank (see Matthew 15:29–30).

When we shift our gaze off our problems and focus on God, we realize that He is big enough, smart enough, good enough, and powerful enough to turn those problems into something good (see Romans 8:28). As Isaiah said to the Lord, "You will keep in perfect peace those whose minds are steadfast, because they trust in you" (Isaiah 26:3).

But the power of prayer extends beyond how it makes us feel. The power of prayer is that it invites God into the situation. It turns the problem over to the One who is big enough to do something about it.

Paul said that when worry starts, shift your focus. Replace worry with worship, praise, and prayer.

Petition. The word *petition* refers to making specific requests to God. The idea is to take what you are worried about and specifically turn it into a prayer request.

Many of our worries involve, as the saying goes, trying to handle tomorrow's problems with today's grace. Therefore, I have found it helpful to go to God in the morning and ask Him to give me my "daily bread" (Matthew 6:11). I ask Him to give me everything I need to face everything that day will bring my way.

Then I obey Peter's encouragement to "cast all your anxiety on him because he cares for you" (1 Peter 5:7). In my journal, I list everything I have to do that day and everything I am tempted to worry about. One by one, I specifically give each activity and each anxiety to God as I ask Him to be active in every area and situation. I cast my cares on God and let Him worry about them that day.

Thanksgiving. This speaks of expressing gratitude to God for what He has done for me in the past and is doing for me in the present. Gratitude and worry are mutually exclusive, meaning both of them can't occupy your mind at the same time. Watch your anxiety level drop when you replace worry with giving thanks to God for all He has done for you. Doing this will strengthen your faith to believe that He can and will do it again.

Worry leads us to see only negatives. When we are filled with worry, we seem to remember only negative events from our past, are staggered by the negatives currently confronting us, and are frozen by the potential negatives looming on the horizon. But thanksgiving causes negatives to shrink.

In another book, I told this story about my friend Sandy:

> I have a friend named Sandy. Seizures have made her unable to work and have put her in the hospital on many occasions. Yet, every time I talk to her she gushes with gratitude. The last time we spoke, she told me her most recent seizure blocked her verbal abilities for a time.
>
> If I were in her shoes, I would be worried about what further losses I might experience, but not Sandy. She uses the power of thanksgiving to replace worry and usher in peace.
>
> When I talked with her about her health issues, she smiled broadly and said, "But it's a blessing."
>
> Then she really floored me when she said, "I am thankful for it because it helped me be a better listener."[2]

3. Experience peace: The goal is to have God's peace replace worry—and it will, through prayer. God is greater than any problem, and His peace can trump any worry.

If anyone was ever in a truly hopeless situation, it was Paul. If anyone had reason to worry, he did. But he didn't. Instead he enjoyed peace. How he could have peace is beyond human understanding. That's the point. Turning worry into prayer brings the peace of God which "transcends all understanding."

Paul wrote that God's peace will "guard your hearts and your minds in Christ Jesus." Hearts and minds are the two places where worry lives. Anxiety can fill our thoughts and overwhelm our hearts. Yet through prayer, God's peace will guard our hearts, acting as a supernatural soldier standing as a sentry and refusing to allow worry to enter our minds or fill our hearts.

Your Twenty-Eight Days to Powerful Prayer

Do you need peace? Are you facing difficult decisions, anxious situations, or tough adversaries? If so, then stop worrying and start praying.

Let me suggest that you write down a list of the things that worry you. As you go through every item on the list, praise the Lord because He is bigger than all your problems put together. Thank God for how He has helped you through similar problems in the past. Turn each one of your problems into prayer requests. Ask Him to take care of them, then leave them with Him and go off in peace.

Questions to Consider

1. What special truth did you learn—or were reminded of—in this chapter?
2. What are three of your biggest worries?
3. What do you intend to do about your worries this week?

Notes

1. "Facts and Statistics" Anxiety and Depression Association https://adaa.org/about-adaa/press-room/facts-statistics (accessed March 10, 2019). Many more agonize with anxiety often.
2. Dave Earley, *The 21 Most Encouraging Promises in the Bible* (Uhrichsville, Ohio: Barbour Publishing, Inc., 2006), 146–147.

THE DAILY PRAYERS

The Prayer of Thanksgiving

They were ten desperate men. The Bible does not tell us whether they had planned to see Jesus that day or if it was just a chance meeting. But it does tell us that ten men with an incurable disease called leprosy met Jesus as He traveled along the border between Samaria and Galilee on His way to Jerusalem (see Luke 17:11–19).

As lepers in the first century, these ten men were cursed to live lives of isolation and humiliation. Because of their disease, they were outcasts. They were forbidden from making any physical contact with other people out of fear that they might spread their disease. Their situation was hopeless because there was no known cure for their leprosy at the time. The disease would gradually consume more and more of their appendages and limbs—until death brought a welcome relief.

To these ten lepers, Jesus was a ray of hope in their dark, desperate lives. People said that He was a mighty healer. They had heard that He had already healed one leper (see Matthew 8:2). Maybe, just maybe, He could heal them.

Here's what happened the day they met Jesus:

> *As he was going into a village, ten men who had leprosy met him. They stood at a distance and called out in a loud voice, "Jesus, Master, have pity on us!"*
> Luke 17:12–13

They were stunned when Jesus responded to them right away:

> When he saw them, he said, "Go, show yourselves to the
> priests." And as they went, they were cleansed.
> LUKE 17:14

I would love to have seen these men's faces and listened to their conversation as they ran down the road to show the priests that they were now "clean." The curse was lifted. They had endured years of loneliness and isolation, years of being shunned. But now they could go home to family and friends. They would not hear any more jokes or ridicule. They had renewed self-respect and dignity. Jesus had given these ten men brand-new lives.

Then, something else happened:

> One of them, when he saw he was healed, came back,
> praising God in a loud voice. He threw himself at Jesus'
> feet and thanked him—and he was a Samaritan.
> LUKE 17:15–16

Ten men had been miraculously healed that day, but only one of them returned to Jesus to thank Him for what He had done. In doing that, this cleansed, healed man set an example for us today.

The Prayer of Thanksgiving

The one grateful former leper went back to Jesus and offered a prayer of thanksgiving—a verbal expression of appreciation to God for His generosity and goodness. It is saying "thank You" for the specific gifts He has given you.

Prayers of thanksgiving are some of the most common prayers of the Bible. Many men and women in the Bible opened their mouths and thanked God for the things He had done for them. Like that one leper who returned to Jesus to thank Him, these people set powerful examples of the power of giving thanks.

Thanksgiving should be a regular part of your prayer adventure. For one thing, gratitude is an indication of humility and the cure for complaining. It is one of the most powerful things you can do as you pray.

The Power of Thanksgiving

In my early thirties, I went through some serious physical issues that eventually led me to make a commitment to offer only prayers of thanksgiving for a period of thirty days—no requests for myself or anyone else, just thanking God for His goodness and all He had done and was doing for me.

After about ten days of only thanksgiving prayers, God began doing some amazing works of healing in me. I was excited to see what God would do for me next.

Then it happened.

"You have to come right away!" the voice on the phone shouted in the middle of the night. "Diane's in the closet with a cord around her neck and says that she'll kill herself if you can't talk her out of it." (No pressure there, right?)

I crawled out of bed and got dressed. Diane and her family lived only a few minutes away. As I drove to their house, I wanted to cry out to God for help, but I was committed to nothing but thanksgiving for another few days.

So I prayed, "God, I thank You for having this under control. I thank You that You will help me and give me wisdom. I thank You that You love Diane and that You will help her tonight."

When I walked into Diane's small house, I felt a heavy, dark cloud of spiritual oppression. Diane was still in the closet and still threatening suicide. I talked with her husband, Mark, and found that this episode was triggered when Mark lost his job. . .again.

I talked with Diane and discovered that this new financial pressure, compounded by the presence of four small children in the home, was more than she thought she could bear. All she saw ahead of her was hopelessness. She could not take it anymore, and this was her desperate cry for help.

I felt a strong prompting from God to give Diane a proposition. I was mostly confident that if she tried to carry out the suicide, we could break down the door and rescue her in time, if it came to that. However, I was still shocked as these words came out of my mouth: "Diane, I'll make you a deal. If we cannot come up with one hundred reasons for you to be thankful, you can go ahead and kill yourself. But if we come up with a hundred reasons for you to be thankful, you have to come out and talk."

What have I done? I thought. *One hundred reasons? We will never make it.*

She cried out, "I am not thankful for anything. I just want to die."

"Not so fast," I said. "First, let us at least try to come up with one hundred reasons to give thanks." I looked at Mark anxiously, hoping he would say something that would help.

"Stacy, Katy, Lyndsey, and Matthew," Mark said, naming their four children. "That's four good reasons to be thankful."

"The fact that we live in a house and not an apartment. You said that just last week," he added. "That's five."

"Did you eat dinner tonight?" I asked. "Many people went to bed hungry tonight."

"Yes," she said.

"That's six!" Mark noted.

"How about having a car?" I asked.

"I am glad my grandma gave us that nice car," Diane whispered.

"That's seven," Mark said.

"How about the cat?" I said, spying a cat in the corner as I looked desperately around the house.

"I love that dumb cat," she said quietly from behind the door.

"Eight," I counted.

"What about your parents?" Mark asked. "They'd be nine and ten."

"And your brother and sister," he added.

"That's twelve," I said, keeping track.

"Plus, your grandma and grandpa. They make fourteen," said Mark.

"Fourteen," I said, smiling now. "Keep going."

Mark looked at me, stumped.

I desperately looked around the sparsely furnished house. "The lamp," I said. "And the couch and the big brown chair."

"Seventeen," Mark said.

"And the TV," I said. "That's eighteen."

"It doesn't work," she snarled angrily.

"Okay, we won't count that one." I said, "How about the end table?"

Mark frowned, shook his head at me, and whispered, "She doesn't like that table."

"I meant the *kitchen* table," I said as I walked into the kitchen.

Mark smiled and nodded.

"And the six kitchen chairs," I said.

"That's twenty-four reasons to be thankful," Mark said.

Only twenty-four? I thought. *We need seventy-six more reasons! We are in big trouble.*

"The blender and the toaster," I said, pointing to the counter.

"The oven and the refrigerator," I added.

"Twenty-eight" Mark said.

We had seventy-two more reasons to go. I was feeling desperate.

Then I opened the refrigerator. It was nearly empty. "The milk, and the ketchup, and the pickles. . .and. . .and the mustard," I said.

Diane giggled quietly from behind the door.

I opened a drawer. "Five measuring spoons, three sharp knives, a strainer," I said naming the things in the drawer. "And a wide, flat thing with a short handle."

"A spatula?" Diane asked.

"That's it, a spatula!"

As Diane began to join in giving reasons to be thankful, the atmosphere in the house changed from despair to delight. Mark and I continued listing everything we could see and giving her reasons to be thankful. By the time we reached number fifty, we were laughing.

Soon after that, the closet door creaked, and Diane came out with a guilty expression on her face. "I am sorry to do this to you," she said. "I don't want to die. I have too much to live for."

Never underestimate the power of thanksgiving.

The Habit of Thanksgiving

When Daniel faced almost certain death in the lions' den because of his faithfulness to the Lord, he was not shaken. He had a holy habit that had served him well throughout his life—thanksgiving:

> *Now when Daniel learned that the decree had been published, he went home to his upstairs room where the windows opened toward Jerusalem. Three times a day he got down on his knees and prayed, giving thanks to his God, just as he had done before.*
> DANIEL 6:10

God responded to Daniel's prayers of thanksgiving in miraculous fashion, going with him into the lions' den, shutting the lions' mouths, and leading him out unharmed. On top of that, Daniel's enemies were executed, and the name of the Lord God was proclaimed throughout the land.

Never underestimate the habit of thanksgiving.

Your Twenty-Eight Days to Powerful Prayer

You can develop your own habit of thanksgiving. During this twenty-eight-day adventure, create a list of one hundred reasons to give thanks.

I like to make my list by sections: Spiritual Blessings, Physical Blessings, Material Blessings, People Who Are Blessings, and Times God Has Blessed Me in the Past. Several times each day, I offer a prayer of thanksgiving for at least five things on my list. Also, at the end of each day, I stop and thank God for three or four blessings He gave me that day.

It sounds simple, and it is. But it's also a huge step toward establishing a powerful life of prayer. So give it a try!

Questions to Consider

1. Do you tend to be more like the one leper who gave thanks or the nine who did not? (Luke 17:11–19)
2. What has God done for you recently that you can thank Him for now?
3. What part of Diane's story do you relate to most?
4. Do you need God to fight some battles for you? (see 2 Chronicles 20:20–27)
5. How can you best invite God into a difficult situation? (see Daniel 6)

THE DAILY PRAYERS

The Prayer of Praise

Have your circumstances ever made you feel trapped? Has someone ever treated you unjustly? Have you lost things you held dear through no fault of your own? Have you ever suffered through an embarrassing situation? Are you facing a ferociously difficult season right now?

If so, you will be able to relate to David, Paul and Silas, and Habakkuk.

Praise in the Cave

David became an instant celebrity among the people of Israel when he bravely killed the Philistine giant Goliath. The people even wrote a song about him: "Saul has killed his thousands, but David his tens of thousands" (1 Samuel 18:7 HCSB).

After bringing down Goliath, David went on a whirlwind ride of one unbelievable success after another. He married King Saul's daughter and dined at the king's table. He became best friends with Saul's son Jonathan. Plus, he was consistently victorious as a military general. He was truly the undisputed darling of the nation.

And jealous King Saul hated David for it.

Saul tried to kill David and failed. Then he ordered Jonathan to kill David, but he refused. So Saul tried to kill David again.

Having no other choice, David left everything and fled for his life. But Saul would not back off. He gathered an army and hunted David through the stark desert wilderness of Judea.

To hide from Saul, David tried to go to the one place Saul would never look for him—Philistine territory. But the Philistine King Achish was understandably suspicious of the man who had killed his greatest warrior. David's only means of escape was to pretend to be insane by scribbling on the walls and slobbering in his beard (1 Samuel 21:10–15). Then Achish exclaimed, "Do I lack madmen?" (1 Samuel 21:15 AMP). When Achish kicked him out, David fled to a cave (1 Samuel 22:1).

The highs and lows in David's life are staggering. He went from being the most popular man in the entire nation to the most wanted. He was humiliated, destitute, misjudged, hated, hunted. . .and hiding in a cave in the middle of nowhere.

How did David respond to such an unfair, awful, embarrassing, terrible turn of events? He offered the prayer of praise:

> I will praise the LORD at all times; His praise will always be on my lips.
> PSALM 34:1 HCSB

Circumstances change, but because God does not change, David determined that his life of praise would not change either. Praise would be a part of his life for all of his life, no matter what. That is why he wrote:

> My heart, O God, is steadfast, my heart is steadfast; I will sing and make music. Awake, my soul! Awake, harp and lyre! I will awaken the dawn. I will praise you, Lord, among the nations; I will sing of you among the peoples. For great is your love, reaching to the heavens; your faithfulness reaches to the skies.
> PSALM 57:7–10

David dealt with his worst days the same way he dealt with his best days. He determined to offer the prayer of praise. In doing so, he set an example for all of us.

Praise in a Prison

The New Testament missionaries Paul and Silas traveled to the Greek city of Philippi hoping to plant a church. Instead, they found themselves in prison.

The two men freed a fortune-telling slave girl from a demon. However, the girl's owner did not appreciate the potential lost income, and he stirred up a crowd and the authorities in Philippi against Paul and Silas. The innocent, well-meaning, church-planting missionaries were mobbed, beaten, and taken to the inner cell of the prison, where their feet were locked in stocks.

Paul and Silas refused the urge to pout and whine, and instead they offered the prayer of praise:

> *About midnight Paul and Silas were praying and singing hymns to God, and the other prisoners were listening to them.*
> Acts 16:25

God obviously heard and enjoyed their prayer of praise. Instead of leaving them in their awful state, He shook things up. . . literally:

> *Suddenly there was such a violent earthquake that the foundations of the prison were shaken. At once all the prison doors flew open, and everyone's chains came loose.*
> Acts 16:26

God sent an earthquake to set the prisoners free. But that's not all. Here's what happened next:

> *The jailer woke up, and when he saw the prison doors open, he drew his sword and was about to kill himself because he thought the prisoners had escaped. But Paul shouted, "Don't harm yourself! We are all here!" The jailer called for lights, rushed in and fell trembling before Paul and Silas. He then brought them out and asked, "Sirs, what must I do to be saved?"*
> Acts 16:27–30

The jailer was so captured by the events he had just witnessed that he wanted to be saved. Paul and Silas did not miss the opportunity to share the gospel:

> They replied, *"Believe in the Lord Jesus, and you will be saved—you and your household."* Then they spoke the word of the Lord to him and to all the others in his house. At that hour of the night the jailer took them and washed their wounds; then immediately he and all his household were baptized.
> Acts 16:31–33

As a seminary professor of evangelism and church planting, I didn't generally teach that getting thrown into jail is the best method of starting churches. But it worked for Paul and Silas. The jailer and his family were influential people in the city of Philippi and good building blocks for the new church.

Praise in difficult times frees God to do God-sized things.

Praise the Lord Anyway

Habakkuk, the Old Testament prophet, was heartbroken over the sin, strife, and oppression of his people. He also had the unenviable task of proclaiming to the people of Judah their coming judgment at the hands of the Babylonians.

How did he face his dark situation?

With a song of praise. He resolved to face the pending painful season with the prayer of praise:

> *Though the fig tree does not blossom and there is no fruit on the vines, though the yield of the olive fails and the fields produce no food, though the flock is cut off from the fold and there are no cattle in the stalls,*
>
> *Yet I will [choose to] rejoice in the Lord; I will [choose to] shout in exultation in the [victorious] God of my salvation!*
>
> *The Lord God is my strength [my source of courage, my invincible*

army]; He has made my feet [steady and sure] like hinds' feet and makes me walk [forward with spiritual confidence] on my high places [of challenge and responsibility].
HABAKKUK 3:17–19 AMP

Habakkuk responded to a fearful forecast with the resolution to praise the Lord anyway. Too often our praise is tied to our feelings, but Habakkuk knew that pure praise is a choice of the will: "Yet I will [choose to] rejoice in the LORD" (Habakkuk 3:18).

Too often our praise is contingent upon our circumstances, but Habakkuk knew that praise is centered on his God. No matter what happens, God does not change, and He is what we need: "The Lord GOD is my strength [my source of courage, my invincible army]" (Habakkuk 3:19 AMP).

Offering the Prayer of Praise

Praise is a positive recognition and appropriate response to the unparalleled person of God. It is a verbal acknowledgment of the character and nature of God. It is the joyous celebration of the greatness and goodness of God.

Praise is found throughout the Bible but is centered in the psalms. The Hebrew word *psalms*, in fact, is the word for "praises" (*Těhillah*). The Book of Psalms uses the word *praise* 189 times. Other words used as synonyms include *extol, proclaim, bless, exalt, glorify, worship, thank, magnify, sing,* and *shout.*

Praise can be said, sung, or shouted. We can praise God with instruments and with dance. We can praise God standing, seated, or facedown. Praise is about action and attitude.

There are many good reasons to praise God. Some of my favorite include the following:

1. Praise frees God to fight our battles for us (2 Chronicles 20:20–24).
2. Praise creates a stronghold that silences the enemy (Psalm 8:2).
3. Praise is where God establishes His rule and reign (Psalm 22:3).

4. Praise is the key into God's courts (Psalm 100:4).
5. Praise helps to replace a spirit of despair (Isaiah 61:3).
6. Praise lifts our eyes off our circumstances and onto our God (Habakkuk 3:17–19).

The Focus of Our Praise

God should always be the focus of our praise. I find it helpful to praise God for some of the different aspects of His character and/or by His special names. Here are some praiseworthy parts of God's nature:

- God is Infinite. He is unlimited.
- God is almighty. He is strong enough.
- God knows everything. He is wise.
- God is everywhere present. He is near.
- God is majestic. He is grand, glorious, regal, and beautiful.
- God is the one and only true God.
- God is sovereign. He does what He wants when He wants.
- God is trustworthy and faithful. You can trust Him.
- God is holy. He is separate from and beyond any and all sin.
- God is loving.
- God is true, righteous, and just.
- God is merciful (He withholds the punishment you deserve).
- God is gracious (He gives blessings you do not deserve).
- God is worthy of worship.

And here are some of God's names and titles:

- Redeemer
- Savior
- Deliverer

- King of kings
- Lord of lords
- Wonderful Counselor
- Mighty God
- Good Shepherd
- Great Physician
- Creator: The Maker of Heaven and Earth

Your Twenty-Eight Days to Powerful Prayer

You can make praise a part of your lifestyle. It may be helpful to add some of these suggestions into your daily life:

1. Use your imagination to picture God as you approach Him. See Him as the great King high and lifted up. Picture Him as your Savior suffering for you on the Cross. Hear Him calming the storm with a simple word. See Him as the Good Shepherd.

2. Listen to praise and worship music often.

3. Every time you sing praise, don't let your mind be filled with a thousand other details. Concentrate on the words. More importantly, picture the One they were written for and sing them as if you are in the throne room of the King of kings Himself, because, in a very real sense, you are (Ephesians 2:4–6).

4. When you participate in corporate worship, do it with all your heart, soul, mind, and strength. Open your mouth. Raise your voice. Lift your hands. Move your feet. Clap your hands.

5. Open every prayer, every day, with at least one sentence praising God by one of His attributes or names.

Questions to Consider

1. Which story resonated most deeply with you: David's, Paul and Silas's, or Habakkuk's? Why?
2. Of the six reasons given for praise in this chapter, which one appeals to you the most? Why?
3. Which of the fourteen attributes of God listed in this chapter most caught your attention?
4. Which of the names of God do you want to remember?
5. How can you make praise a larger part of your life?

DAY 10

The Prayer of Confession and Heart Cleansing

Carl, my father-in-law, looked very healthy for a seventy-two-year-old man. He was slim and trim and lived an active life. But one night we got a call telling us that Carl had suffered a stroke.

The doctors examined Carl and discovered that he had several blocked arteries and needed an operation. When the surgeons opened him up, however, they found that they could not complete the surgery as planned because Carl's heart was blocked by a cancerous tumor, and he also had cancer in his lungs.

No one knew he had cancer until they had opened his chest for surgery.

The Bible clearly states that we live on a sin-cursed planet and that all of us have a sin nature. It is easy for our hearts to develop potentially dangerous spiritual diseases that take root and eat us up like cancer. Bitterness, selfishness, pride, rebellion, anxiety, fear, greed, envy, lust, idolatry, and worldliness are devastating "heart diseases" that must be removed through the cleansing that comes through confession (1 John 1:9) and the Word (John 15:3).

Heart Searching

King David was a man after God's own heart (1 Samuel 13:14; Acts 13:22), but later in his life, he learned that he could not trust his own heart. He knew from painful failure that even though things may appear healthy on the outside, there could be disease within. So, David offered a prayer inviting the Lord to examine his heart:

> Search me, God, and know my heart; test me and know my anxious thoughts. See if there is any offensive way in me, and lead me in the way everlasting.
> PSALM 139:23–24

It takes courage to open our hearts and lives to the scrutiny of the "Heart Surgeon." But it is worth it, as it leads to our hearts being cleansed, healed, liberated, comforted, and changed.

Have you ever had the courage to invite God to examine your heart? When was the last time you asked God to reveal where bitterness had taken root, or where selfishness and pride had begun to block the life of God from flowing through you? When did you last ask God to search your heart of rebellion, anxiety, fear, greed, envy, lust, or worldliness? How long has it been since you allowed God to perform heart surgery?

Several times a year, I take time away from people to get alone with God and allow Him to search my heart. When I am feeling brave, I go through a spiritual inventory list that makes me look into areas I am naturally reluctant to search.

Four Tests

Below are four lists of scripture-based questions that can serve as rigorous tests of the heart. As you read through these, ask the Holy Spirit to search your heart for potentially cancerous sins. When the Holy Spirit points out a sin, confess it and ask God to cleanse your heart of that matter.

THE TEST OF THE TEN COMMANDMENTS (EXODUS 20:3–17)

1. Am I putting anything or anyone above my relationship with God?
2. Do I have idols in my life?

3. Have I misused the Lord's name?
4. Do I give God a day of the week—the time He deserves?
5. Am I honoring my father and mother?
6. Do I have anger in my heart toward another?
7. Have I committed sexually lustful acts or had sexually lustful thoughts?
8. Have I stolen anything, such as money or time, from anyone, including God?
9. Have I failed to tell the truth? Have I attempted to deceive someone?
10. Have I coveted anything belonging to someone else—a possession, a position, or a relationship?

THE TEST OF THE GREAT COMMANDMENT, PART 1 (MATTHEW 22:37)

1. Am I loving God with all my heart, soul, mind, and strength?
2. Am I loving God with all of my heart or only part?
3. Am I loving God first above all others?
4. Am I loving God fervently?
5. Are there people, or things, I love more than I love God?
6. Do my choices and actions reflect love for God?
7. Does the way I use my time each day reveal that I love God more than other things?

THE TEST OF THE GREAT COMMANDMENT, PART 2 (MATTHEW 22:37)

1. Am I loving my neighbors as myself?
2. Do I know my neighbors' names? Do I know their needs?
3. Do my actions testify of my love for others?
4. Am I being exclusive or partial in whom I show love to?
5. Do I think of myself more than I think of others?
6. What do I need to change in order to love others more?
7. To whom should I go out of my way to show love today?

THE TEST OF THE SPIRIT-FILLED LIFE (GALATIANS 6:22–23)

1. Is my life filled with unconditional love for others?
2. Do I have joy even when life is difficult?

3. Do I have peace regardless of my circumstances?
4. Am I a patient person?
5. Do I do kind things for others?
6. Do I love morally good things?
7. Am a I person of faith or of fear?
8. Do I fight against God or am I under His control?
9. Am I growing in self-control and self-discipline?

Heart Cleansing through Confession

It is good to let the Lord examine our hearts and show us our sin. But we must take the next step and allow our sorrow over that sin lead us to confession.

In midlife, King David wasted a year by living in guilt over his sin with Bathsheba. When he finally got serious about dealing with it, he was painfully sorry for it and offered this powerful prayer of confession:

> Have mercy on me, O God, according to your unfailing love; according to your great compassion blot out my transgressions. Wash away all my iniquity and cleanse me from my sin. For I know my transgressions, and my sin is always before me. Against you, you only, have I sinned and done what is evil in your sight; so you are right in your verdict and justified when you judge. Surely I was sinful at birth, sinful from the time my mother conceived me. Yet you desired faithfulness even in the womb; you taught me wisdom in that secret place. Cleanse me with hyssop, and I will be clean; wash me, and I will be whiter than snow. Let me hear joy and gladness; let the bones you have crushed rejoice. Hide your face from my sins and blot out all my iniquity. Create in me a pure heart, O God, and renew a steadfast spirit within me.
> PSALM 51:1–10

In this psalm, David asked for forgiveness and cleansing. In his emotional plea he used every phrase he could think of:

- "Have mercy on me"
- "Blot out my transgressions"
- "Wash away all my iniquity"
- "Cleanse me from my sin"
- "Cleanse me with hyssop"
- "Wash me"
- "Hide your face from my sins"
- "Blot out all my iniquity"

Heart-cleansing prayer happens when we see our sin as God sees it. It is letting the pain our sin causes the Father and Jesus on the Cross fill our thoughts, stir our emotions, and change our wills. It is admitting our sin and agreeing with God that it is wrong and spiritually lethal. And it is allowing God to forgive us and cleanse us:

> *If we confess our sins, he is faithful and just and will forgive us*
> *our sins and purify us from all unrighteousness.*
> 1 JOHN 1:9

The word *confess* literally means "to say the same thing." We are to say the same thing about our sin that *God* says about it. Confessing sin is not merely calling it a "mistake," a "mess-up," an "error," or "misbehavior." It is calling sin, *sin*. It is acknowledging that it must be forgiven. It is asking God to wash it off our record and purify our hearts:

> *Whoever conceals their sins does not prosper, but the one who*
> *confesses and renounces them finds mercy.*
> PROVERBS 28:13

Sin is unconquered until it is uncovered. Heart-cleansing prayer starts with refusing to deny the reality of your sin before God. It is uncovering your sin and confessing it so that God may grant you mercy and give you victory over it.

Accept Forgiveness

The goal of this day's adventure is not to leave you curled up in the corner in a fetal position, crushed by guilt. It is to help you experience a deeper level of joy (Psalm 51:8, 12) and a higher level of passion (Psalm 51:10, 12).

However, it is not enough to ask God to examine our hearts and point out sin. It is not enough to confess that sin. We must also *accept God's forgiveness* for it. The word *forgive* essentially means "to cancel a debt, delete an offense, and to wipe the record clean."

God is merciful and wants to forgive us, but He is also just and must punish sin. He is able to forgive us because the sinless blood of Jesus paid for our sins (1 Peter 1:18–19).

When we sincerely confess our sins, God looks at the price Jesus paid so that we can be forgiven, and He says it was more than good enough. He declares that we are no longer guilty.

Slowly read these great promises:

For as high as the heavens are above the earth, so great is his love for those who fear him; as far as the east is from the west, so far has he removed our transgressions from us.
PSALM 103:11–12

"Come now, let us settle the matter," says the LORD. "Though your sins are like scarlet, they shall be as white as snow; though they are red as crimson, they shall be like wool."
ISAIAH 1:18

"I, even I, am he who blots out your transgressions, for my own sake, and remembers your sins no more."
ISAIAH 43:25

You will again have compassion on us; you will tread our sins underfoot and hurl all our iniquities into the depths of the sea.
MICAH 7:19

Your Twenty-Eight Days to Powerful Prayer

There are two primary ways to apply this chapter. First, make confession of sins a part of your daily prayer time. Just as you cleanse your body daily by taking a shower, cleanse your heart by confessing every attitude, word, and action you know displeases the Lord.

Second, just as you set aside a special time to do a deep "spring cleaning" of your house, set aside an opportunity to regularly give extended prayer time for deep cleansing. Ask the Holy Spirit to examine your heart and point out sins. Confess those sins and accept God's forgiveness.

Questions to Consider

1. What did you learn from this chapter?
2. Did you take all four of the heart-searching tests? Which one did you find most convicting?
3. What sin do you need to uncover before God?
4. What sin do you need to confess to God today?
5. How will you apply this chapter to your life of prayer?

THE DAILY PRAYERS

The Prayer of Supplication

God has revealed Himself to us with a multitude of attributes and names, each reflecting a different aspect of His glorious nature. Because prayer is the primary way we connect our hearts with God's heart, it also expresses itself in a variety of ways, such as:

- Conversing with God
- Hearing God's voice
- Declaring God's worth and praising Him for who He is
- Expressing gratitude to God for all He has done
- Allowing the Holy Spirit to examine your heart
- Confessing sin
- Surrendering every aspect of your life to God
- Forgiving those who have sinned against you
- Exercising authority over the enemy
- Asking God to meet your needs

It is important to develop a well-rounded prayer life. But we need to realize that the central meaning of prayer is *asking*. Yes, we should praise God because He is worth it. Yes, we need to thank God for all He has so generously given us. Yes, we must confess our sins because God is holy. Yes, we must forgive those who sin against us, for He forgives us. And yes, we ought to surrender every aspect of our lives to God because He is Lord.

However, we should also *ask God our Father to meet our needs*. We will always be dependent upon God. Therefore, we should always come to Him, asking Him to meet our needs. The words used most often for "prayer" in both the Old and New Testament have the primary meaning of *asking*. Why? Because, as I pointed out in Day 5, prayer is primarily asking.

The Prayer of Supplication

The prayer of supplication means asking God to *meet* a specific need. It is petitioning the throne of the King of kings. It is making a request of your heavenly Father. It is asking God to do what no one else can do and expecting Him to do it. The prayer of supplication is simply asking, and the answer to the prayer of supplication is receiving.

The disciples asked Jesus, "Teach us to pray" (Luke 11:1). In response, Jesus gave the popular prayer outline most of us call the Lord's Prayer and scholars call the Disciples' Prayer or the Model Prayer (Luke 11:2–4). The heart of this prayer is a series of requests:

- "Father, hallowed be your name"
- "Your kingdom come"
- "Give us each day our daily bread"
- "Forgive us our sins"
- "Lead us not into temptation"

When Jesus taught His disciples to pray, therefore, He taught them to make requests to the Father for important things.

Boldly Asking

After Jesus gave the Disciples' Prayer, He told a story about a man asking his friend for bread and receiving it because of his bold persistence:

Then Jesus said to them, "Suppose you have a friend, and you go to him at midnight and say, 'Friend, lend me three loaves of bread; a friend of mine on a journey has come to me, and I

have no food to offer him.' And suppose the one inside answers, 'Don't bother me. The door is already locked, and my children and I are in bed. I can't get up and give you anything.' I tell you, even though he will not get up and give you the bread because of friendship, yet because of your shameless audacity he will surely get up and give you as much as you need."
Luke 11:5–8

The man received bread because he had boldly asked his friend for it. Jesus followed His story of the man asking and receiving bread from his friend with a promise regarding prayer as asking and receiving:

"So, I say to you: Ask and it will be given to you; seek and you will find; knock and the door will be opened to you. For everyone who asks receives; the one who seeks finds; and to the one who knocks, the door will be opened. Which of you fathers, if your son asks for a fish, will give him a snake instead? Or if he asks for an egg, will give him a scorpion? If you then, though you are evil, know how to give good gifts to your children, how much more will your Father in heaven give the Holy Spirit to those who ask him!"
Luke 11:9–13

Note that the word *ask* appears in each of the five verses of the above passage. That shows us that the requirement for receiving is asking. The answer to asking is receiving.

Yes, prayer makes us feel better. Yes, prayer refocuses our minds, hearts, and priorities. Yes, prayer lifts our gaze to God. But prayer also gets answers. It is God's way of building our relationship with Him as we come to Him with our needs and He comes to us by meeting those needs.

They Asked and Received

In the Bible, when people prayed, they asked God for things. Here are some of the many short, simple prayers of people asking God for things:

- Abraham's servant, as he tried to find a wife for Isaac, asked, "Make me successful today" (Genesis 24:12).
- Jacob, as he wrestled with the Lord, said, "Bless me" (Genesis 32:26).
- Hannah pleaded, "Remember me" (1 Samuel 1: 11).
- David prayed, "Wash me. . .cleanse me" (Psalm 51:7).
- Solomon prayed, "Give me wisdom, that I may lead this people" (2 Chronicles 1:10).
- Jabez requested, "Bless me and enlarge my territory!" (1 Chronicles 4:10).
- When Elijah needed fire from heaven to shake the nation of Israel, he prayed, "Answer me" (1 Kings 18:37).
- As he faced imminent defeat, King Hezekiah begged God, "Deliver us" (2 Kings 19:19).
- In a circumstance similar to the one Hezekiah faced, Asa asked, "Help us" (2 Chronicles 14:11).
- When Nehemiah needed the king's blessing to rebuild the walls around Jerusalem, he prayed, "Give your servant success" (Nehemiah 1:11).
- When Nehemiah faced tremendous opposition in the task, he prayed, "Strengthen my hands" (Nehemiah 6:9).
- The young prophet requested, "Send me" (Isaiah 6:8).
- As they faced what seemed like certain death on the Sea of Galilee during a storm, the disciples prayed, "Lord, save us" (Matthew 8:25).
- The blind men cried out, "Have mercy on us" (Matthew 9:27).
- The tax collector said, "God, have mercy on me, a sinner" (Luke 18:13).
- The thief prayed, "Remember me when you come into your kingdom" (Luke 23:42).
- Jesus said, "Father, forgive them" (Luke 23:34).

All of these prayers are short, plain, simple petitions to the Father to supply a specific need, and all of them were marvelously answered. Every one of them resulted in people receiving what they asked for—and, in many cases, *more* than they asked for.

Prayer is asking and receiving. When we ask God for things, we should expect Him to answer these requests.

How to Ask More Effectively

Here are some keys to asking more effectively as you pray:

1. *Filter your requests*: Jesus taught that we are to ask for things that exalt God's name, advance God's kingdom, or accomplish God's will.

2. *Feel free to ask for the things that supply your needs*: Ask God to meet *your* needs—daily bread, forgiveness, direction, protection (Luke 11:2–4; Matthew 6:9–13). Jesus wants us to bring our every need and every desire to our heavenly Father.

3. *Realize that if it is good to have, it is good to ask for*: I used to be hesitant to ask God for things because I did not want to be selfish or trivial, but I have changed my position. Now I contend that if it is good for you to have, it is good to ask for. God is honored when we bring everything that is important to us to His attention.

4. *It is okay to ask for small things*: I am a better buyer than a shopper. Some people like to shop, but I am not one of those people. When I shop, my mind is bombarded with a hundred other things I should be doing. So I much prefer to go into a store, grab what I need, try it on if necessary, buy it, and leave.

Therefore, I try to make shopping a spiritual endeavor. I attempt to get a clear understanding of what I need and where it will be found. When I get there, I ask the Holy Spirit to guide me to what I need quickly and simply. I ask Him to guide me to the best buy possible. Then I head out into the store to buy it.

Sure enough, almost every time, He answers my prayer. Occasionally, He will trump my request and slow me down because someone needed encouragement or a listening ear. But when I make prayer a part of my shopping experience, it is remarkably quick, easy, and painless. It may be a small thing, but it is important to me and He answers.

Your Twenty–Eight Days to Powerful Prayer

I encourage you to take some time each day and ask God to supply the things you really need and want. It is right to let God know exactly what is on your heart. I usually make a list of the big things I am asking for daily and the things I need for that specific day.

I also suggest that you pray throughout the day about "little" things: "Help me know what to say right now," "Give me wisdom," "Guide me," "Help me keep my mouth shut." You may be surprised at how He answers these little prayers for you.

Questions to Consider

1. What in this chapter surprised you about asking and receiving?
2. What prayer for yourself have you seen God answer recently?
3. What will you do to apply this chapter to your prayer life?

THE DAILY PRAYERS

The Prayer of Intercession

Are there people in your life who have large needs? Has some-one you love wandered far from God? Do you wish you knew what to say when you pray for others? Would you like to be more effective when you pray for others?

If you answered any of these questions "Yes," take time to learn about the prayer of intercession. Jesus will be your teacher.

Jesus the Intercessor

Jesus was a great teacher, a powerful miracle worker, a tender healer, a victorious warrior, and the perfect, selfless, sacrificial Savior. But of those impressive roles, Jesus is right now fulfilling one primary responsibility—He is our intercessor.

Intercession is standing in the gap between God and man by asking God to extend grace and mercy. It is active advocacy. Jesus invested Himself by leaving heaven to come to earth. He fully identified with us by becoming one of us. He stood in for us when He took the punishment for our sin on the Cross. Today He advocates in prayer every day as He appeals to the Father on our behalf.

In Jesus' great High Priestly Prayer for His disciples, He made this definitive statement of an intercessor: "I pray for them" (John 17:9). He was about to be arrested, tried, beaten, whipped, mocked, and crucified. Yet, He prayed for His disciples.

He also prayed for us. Speaking of His future followers, He said, "I pray also for those who will believe in me through their message" (John 17:20).

It is great to know that at this very moment, as Jesus sits at the right hand of the Father in heaven, He is not condemning us but interceding for us to the Father:

> Who then is the one who condemns? No one. Christ Jesus who died—more than that, who was raised to life—is at the right hand of God and is also interceding for us.
> ROMANS 8:34

The Bible says that Jesus appeals to the Father on our behalf on the basis of His perfect sacrifice for us on the Cross:

> My dear children, I write this to you so that you will not sin. But if anybody does sin, we have an advocate with the Father—Jesus Christ, the Righteous One. He is the atoning sacrifice for our sins, and not only for ours but also for the sins of the whole world.
> 1 JOHN 2:1–2

Jesus is currently fulfilling His high priestly ministry by interceding in prayer for us:

> Because Jesus lives forever, he has a permanent priesthood. Therefore he is able to save completely those who come to God through him, because he always lives to intercede for them.
> HEBREWS 7:24–25

What does all that mean? First, we can sleep at night in peace and confidence, knowing that Jesus has our backs before the throne of God. Second, we can be encouraged all day long because Jesus, the Son of God, the Lord of all, prays for us.

That means that right this second, Jesus is praying for you! It also means that if we want to follow Jesus' example, we will pray for others. This further means that we can add our prayers to His prayers as He prays for others.

The Prayer of Intercession

Dick Eastman once described intercessory prayer as "Love on its knees."[1] The word *intercede* means "to go between." The prayer of intercession describes the act of going to God and pleading on behalf of another. "Prayer" as a general term describes talking to God, but intercession is more specific. It describes coming to God *on behalf of another*. Therefore, while all intercession is prayer, not all prayer is intercession.[2]

What and Why to Pray for Others

Most of the apostle Paul's intercessory prayers for others were centered more on their *spiritual* condition than their material, physical, temporal needs. (For more on what to pray for others, see Day 23).

Jesus' intercessory prayer for Peter was for faith to be resilient (Luke 22:31–32). He also prayed for His disciples' spiritual protection (John 17:11), unity (John 17:11), joy (John 17:13), and that the Father would sanctify them through the truth of His Word (John 17:17). Jesus focused His prayers for His followers on their spiritual needs.

We also see intercessory prayers in the Bible for people to receive healing, victory, and rescuing mercy.

Praying for others is a great privilege and a necessary obligation. Too often, we view it as optional, but intercessory prayer is our primary role in the body of Christ. Paul urged, "First of all, that petitions, prayers, intercession and thanksgiving be made for all people" (1 Timothy 2:1–2). Jesus commanded us to pray for our enemies "who persecute you" (Matthew 5:44). James said that we are to "pray for each other" (James 5:16).

As a holy priesthood (1 Peter 2:5), a royal priesthood (1 Peter 2:9), and a kingdom of priests (Revelation 1:5), our major role as New Covenant believers is intercession on behalf of others. When we exercise this priestly office by praying for others, we link our hearts with Jesus, the great High Priest, who does the same. We partner with Jesus in bringing the needs of others to our Father's throne.

Praying for others can play a role in their salvation. The great Puritan preacher Charles Spurgeon said:

Many of us trace our conversion, if we go to the root of it, to the prayers of certain godly persons. In innumerable instances the prayers of parents have availed to bring young people to Christ. Many more will have to bless God for praying teachers, praying friends, praying pastors. Obscure persons confined to their beds are often the means of saving hundreds by their continual pleadings with God.[3]

God loves to answer our prayers when we pray for others. James wrote that such prayers of a righteous person are "powerful and effective" (James 5:16). Reading through biblical examples of intercession reveals that praying for others has produced many significant results:

- Because of Abraham's intercessory prayers, the Lord would have spared sinful Sodom. . .*if* there were only ten righteous people there (Genesis 18:20–33).
- Moses' selfless intercession for the rebellious Israelites caused the Lord to change His mind and not destroy them (Exodus 32:9–14).
- Fire fell from heaven in response to Elijah's pleas for God to reveal Himself to Israel (1 Kings 18:36–39).
- God provided the opportunity and resources for Nehemiah to rebuild the walls around Jerusalem after he interceded for the city (Nehemiah 1:4).
- Peter's shattered confidence was powerfully restored because of Jesus' prayer for him (Luke 22:31–32; Acts 2:14–41).
- Peter had the faith to pray for Dorcas, and as a result she was brought back to life (Acts 9:36–41).
- The church prayed for Peter, and as a result, an angel quietly freed him from prison unnoticed (Acts 12:5–17).

Because intercession is the heart and ministry of Jesus, the Father often blesses the intercessor. The story of Job indicates this: "After Job had prayed for his friends, the LORD restored his fortunes and gave him twice as much as he had before" (Job 42:10).

How to Intercede More Effectively

You have seen that God calls us all to be intercessors, to stand in the gap on behalf of others. But how can we do that effectively? Here are some suggestions:

1. *Recognize the privilege you enjoy, the position you hold, the promises you have been given, and the power you wield as an intercessor.* We are privileged to partner with Christ. We are positioned with Him in the heavens at the right hand of the Father. We have been given many promises of answered prayers. And we have been given authority to join God in making things happen on earth for the sake of others.

2. *Ask the Father to guide you as you pray for others.* I find it helpful to ask the Father to give me His heart for the people I am praying for. I also ask Him to help me pray what Jesus is praying for them.

3. *Pray for them as fervently as you would want someone praying for you.*

4. *Plead appropriate Bible promises or pray appropriate scriptures for the one(s) you are praying for.*

5. *Focus on one area each day.* I pray for my immediate family members every day. But I usually don't have time or opportunity to pray for everyone or everything I want to pray for every day. Therefore, I often focus on a different area of intercession each day. For example:

- Sunday: Members of my extended family
- Monday: My friends and neighbors
- Tuesday: The lost
- Wednesday: My fellow spiritual leaders
- Thursday: My government leaders

- Friday: Missionaries and church planters
- Saturday: My church and its upcoming worship services

6. *Be willing to be the answer to your prayers.* There have been times when I have been praying for someone and I sense a need to reach out to that person right away. A surprising number of times, the person has responded by saying something like, "How did you know that I was struggling right now?"

Your Twenty-Eight Days to Powerful Prayer

If you do not regularly intercede for others, why not start today? Add a few minutes of intercession to your prayers each day. Develop a plan to pray for different groups of people on different days of the week. And when a person comes to mind during the day, quickly say a short prayer for them.

Questions to Consider

1. What jumped out at you as you read this chapter? Why?
2. Were you surprised to learn about Jesus the intercessor?
3. What can you take from this chapter to strengthen your intercessory prayer life?

Notes

1. Dick Eastman, *No Easy Road* (Grand Rapids, Michigan: Baker Book House, 1971), 58.
2. C. Peter Wagner, *Prayer Shield* (Ventura, California: Regal Books, 1992), 26.
3. C. H. Spurgeon, from the sermon "Samuel, An Example of Intercession," Delivered on Lord's-Day Morning, May 9th, 1880, bible.org/seriespage/samuel-example-intercession-no-1537, accessed April 5, 2019.

THE DAILY PRAYERS

The Prayer of Surrender

On the night Jesus was arrested, He and the eleven remaining disciples (Judas had already left them and betrayed Jesus) departed from the upper room, where they had shared the Passover meal, and made their way to their usual camping spot in the Garden of Gethsemane. The garden was located at the foot of the Mount of Olives, and it overlooked the city of Jerusalem. Olives were taken to Gethsemane, where they were crushed in wooden presses to produce the olive oil used in the first century for many aspects of daily life.

It was a fitting location, as Jesus grasped a crushing realization.

When they arrived at the garden, Jesus took Peter, James, and John and left the others behind as they traveled a little further. He was about to pray the most wrenching prayer in the entire Bible:

> Then Jesus went with his disciples to a place called Gethsemane, and he said to them, "Sit here while I go over there and pray." He took Peter and the two sons of Zebedee along with him, and he began to be sorrowful and troubled. Then he said to them, "My soul is overwhelmed with sorrow to the point of death. Stay here and keep watch with me."
> MATTHEW 26:36–38

Jesus was looking at more than mere death. He was about to experience intense physical anguish and torture. He would suffer agonizing emotional rejection, denial, and abandonment. Plus, the enemy would be given freedom to assault Him.

Beyond all of that, Jesus faced something no human has ever endured. He was about to pay the awful, immense, costly price to be an offering for the sin of the whole world. He would drink the cup of the wrath of a Holy God poured out against the sins of the entire human race. To accomplish that, His body, soul, and spirit would be ripped apart. Jesus, the eternal Son, would be separated from the heavenly Father. The holy union that stretched from eternity past was about to be severed. He would have to experience the supreme level of punishment and hell as He sacrificed Himself for our sins.

And He did not want to do it.

As Christians, we are rightfully enamored with the fact that Jesus is God. But we often downplay the reality of His humanity. We forget that He emptied Himself and set aside the glories of the godhead to become one of us so that He could die for us (Philippians 2:5–11). Because He made it *look* so easy, we think it *was* easy for Jesus. But it was not.

As a strong-willed individual, I am fascinated by the battle of the wills that Jesus faced in the Garden. I am also deeply challenged by His prayer of surrender.

"Not As I Will"

I am sure that one day in heaven we will be able to investigate everything that went on that night in the Garden of Gethsemane. On one side, Jesus must have felt that He had done enough. He had obeyed the call of God to leave His home in Nazareth and had spent the past four years travelling the country preaching the kingdom of God. As a result, His siblings thought He was crazy and the religious leaders wanted Him dead.

Yet, the Father demanded more. He asked Jesus to become more than the martyr for a movement. He called Him to die as the sacrificial atoning Lamb of God whose blood was needed to redeem sinners back to Him. He wanted Jesus, who in His righteousness had never sinned, to become sin for us in order to make us right with God (1 Corinthians 5:20). He asked Jesus to experience the multiplied hell of every sinner who would ever live. The physical, emotional, mental, and spiritual pain would exceed anything anyone had or would ever know.

Jesus responded humbly and honestly. He also responded with a heart that was surrendered to the will of the Father:

> Going a little farther, he fell with his face to the ground and prayed, "My Father, if it is possible, may this cup be taken from me. Yet not as I will, but as you will."
> MATTHEW 26:39

> He went away a second time and prayed, "My Father, if it is not possible for this cup to be taken away unless I drink it, may your will be done." When he came back, he again found them sleeping, because their eyes were heavy. So he left them and went away once more and prayed the third time, saying the same thing.
> MATTHEW 26:42–44

We dare not think that Jesus' prayer of surrender to the will of the Father was a small thing. It was the most agonizing act any human can perform, and it showed:

> An angel from heaven appeared to him and strengthened him. And being in anguish, he prayed more earnestly, and his sweat was like drops of blood falling to the ground.
> LUKE 22:43–44

These words of surrender were overwhelmingly difficult for Jesus to utter. They were also supremely significant. Because He surrendered, we can be saved.

Surrender Is Necessary

The will of the Father and the will of the Son crossed over the Cross. The Father wanted Jesus to drink the awful cup of suffering in order to save sinners, but Jesus hoped to be relieved of such pending anguish. In the end, Jesus surrendered to the Father's will.

The prayer of surrender involves yielding our entire will to God, much the same way Jesus did in the Garden. This kind of prayer is marked by:

- Choosing God's will over our own will
- Doing what God wants even when we don't want to
- Accepting God's way as better than our own
- Dying to something we hold dear so that God may bring it back to life and bless it, if and how He so desires (see Genesis 22)
- Giving permission for the seed to be put in the ground to die so that it may bring forth a multiplied harvest (see John 12:24–25)
- Letting go of what we deem good so that the Father may give us what He knows is best
- Using the key that frees us from the prison of self

It has been said, "To applaud the will of God, to do the will of God, even fight for the will of God is not difficult. . .until it comes at cross-purposes with our will."[1] But that is what God calls us to do in prayer.

I Surrender

Part of my testimony is the time in my life when I was running from God.

Growing up attending church, I spent my early adolescent years unwilling to fully surrender to God. As a result, I was miserable. I could not enjoy sin, self, rebellion, or the world. Yet, I refused to embrace God or yield to His will over mine.

Eventually I began to grow weary of running and frustrated with fighting.

A Christian friend was wearing me down by inviting me to

church. Deep inside, I longed for the spiritual life he enjoyed.

One Sunday morning, I was sitting in the very back row of the balcony at church. Instead of listening to the message, I was reading a Sunday school paper on my way to a nap. But a little quote jumped off the page and grabbed my attention: "Commitment to God is simply giving all you know of yourself to all you know of God."

I could do that! I thought. *God is much smarter than I am. Maybe I could really commit my life to Him.*

That night, I went to the Bible study for our church's high school students. My friend had been bugging me to go for a while, so I went. That whole evening, God spoke directly to me about surrender. I had some choices to make:

- Would I commit all I knew of myself to all I knew of God?
- Would I surrender my will to His will for my life?
- Would I quit running *from* God and begin to run *to* and *with* Him?

I was afraid of making another emotional decision that would not last, so I resisted making any commitments during the meeting. After I went home, though, I could not take it anymore. I got alone so I could—as an act of the will beyond my emotions—surrender my life fully to God.

I said to God, "From this moment on, I surrender my will to Your will. I commit all I know of me to all I know of You. I give You my past, present, and future. My life is a blank contract before You. My relationships, interests, talents, hopes, dreams, and future belong to You."

I was immediately staggered by the sense of peace that flooded my soul. It was as though a very deep well of joy was opened in my heart. I knew I had done the right thing. People tell me that I smiled for the next two weeks after that night.

That was years ago, but even now, at least once a week, I try to offer a "surrender prayer" to God. I take the biggest areas of my life (my wife, my kids, my grandkids, my ministry, my health, my finances, my material things, my time, my talents, my future) and give them to Him. I pray something like this:

Father in heaven, I give each of these things to You. Do with them as You see fit. I have often told You what I desire to happen in these areas, but not my will but Your will be done. You know what is best. I trust You to accomplish what You know to be best. Amen.

Your Twenty-Eight Days to Powerful Prayer

It is not always easy to surrender everything to God. But when it has been especially hard for me to yield something over to Him, I often see Him increase His activity in these areas *after* I surrender them to Him.

Do you want to see the same thing happen in your life? You can start by creating your own list of ten areas of life you know you need to surrender to God:

1.
2.
3.
4.
5.
6.
7.
8.
9.
10.

Questions to Consider

1. What are three things that impressed you as we looked at Jesus' prayer at Gethsemane?
2. When did you surrender your life completely to God?

3. What are you struggling to surrender to Him right now?
4. Do you make a prayer of surrender a consistent part of your prayer adventure?

Notes

1. Richard Foster, *Prayer: Finding the Heart's True Home* (San Francisco: Harper Collins Publishers, 1992), 50.

THE DAILY PRAYERS

The Prayer of Liberation

Jesus was hurting.

Judas had betrayed Him, Peter had denied Him, and His closest friends had deserted Him.

Jesus had given over three years of His life to loving, teaching, healing, and feeding needy people. Yet those same people cried out for His death with the harsh words, "Crucify Him! Crucify Him!"

The Jewish leaders plotted Jesus' death, Pilate ordered it, and the Romans carried it out. The cruel Roman soldiers beat Him, spit on Him, drove a crown of thorns into His head, and shredded His back with thirty-nine lashes from a brutal leather whip.

Then, in the most grotesque form of execution available, the soldiers drove spikes into His hands and feet, nailing them to crossed pieces of wood. They hung Him up as a spectacle before a jeering crowd.

Writhing in agony, Jesus, the giver of life, had to fight through excruciating pain for every breath as He pulled and pushed against the spikes. Every movement was merciless torture.

Beyond that, the thief beside Him mocked and scorned Him, the crowd viciously derided Him, and the religious leaders jeered at Him with contempt.

All of these people had hurt Jesus, but He did not bow to bitterness. He refused to take His revenge. He did not acquiesce to anger.

Jesus' hands and feet were bound, but not His soul. He resisted the urge to let bitterness take His soul captive. Instead, He prayed the prayer of setting captives free: "Father, forgive them, for they do not know what they are doing" (Luke 23:34).

The Cancelled Debt and the Prison of Bitterness

One day, Peter the disciple came to Jesus with a question regarding the extent of forgiveness. Jesus answered by telling him a story about the unconditional nature of true forgiveness and the power of setting captives free (Matthew 18:21–35).

The story was about a king who did an audit of his books and found that one of his employees had embezzled a massive amount of money from him. His debt was equal to the total amount of taxes Rome collected from four provinces over an eleven-year period![1] This was a huge debt, far more than the man would ever be able to repay.

The indebted man begged for forgiveness, and the merciful king did the unexpected, cancelling the entire debt and setting the man free.

The forgiven man, however, responded by auditing his own books and finding that a poor man owed him a tiny debt, equivalent to several thousand dollars.[2] But the debt was larger than the poor man could repay. When confronted, the poor man begged for forgiveness.

You would think that the man who had just been so fabulously forgiven such a massive debt would graciously forgive the poor man the relatively insignificant debt. But not so. Instead of forgiving the man and setting him free, the forgiven man had the poor man thrown into debtors' prison.

Some of the king's other servants saw the incredible injustice that had occurred, and they reported it to the merciful king. He was infuriated:

> *"Then the master called the servant in. 'You wicked servant,' he said, 'I canceled all that debt of yours because you begged me to. Shouldn't you have had mercy on your fellow servant just*

as I had on you?' In anger his master handed him over to the jailers to be tortured, until he should pay back all he owed."
MATTHEW 18:32–34

This parable teaches us several important truths:

- First, the king in the story is a word picture of a God who has forgiven us a debt far greater than we could ever repay.
- Second, the forgiven man in the story represents each of us. We have received the astounding forgiveness of God, but there are times when we refuse to forgive others of the comparably smaller debts others owe us.
- Third, as we consider the monumental amount of debt from which God has forgiven us, we should be motivated to forgive others.
- Fourth, failing to forgive others places us in captivity.

Bitterness is bondage. It chains us to our enemies and makes us their prisoner. Instead of imprisoning the person we resent, bitterness imprisons us. The prison of bitterness does not have visible shackles and bars, but in many ways it is just as binding as being held in a literal prison cell.

Bitterness toward others makes you *their* prisoner because even when they are not around or thinking about you, you cannot get them out of your mind. The mention of their names can flood your mind with ugly thoughts. Spotting them across a room elevates your heart rate and blood pressure. Hearing their voices makes you wince and cringe. Your bitterness toward *them* tortures *you*.

There is only one way out of the rotten dungeon that is resentment—the prayer that sets captives free.

The Prayer of Liberation
The prayer of liberation is offered on behalf of "enemies." It is a higher expression of love as you "do good to those who hate

you, bless those who curse you, [and] pray for those who mistreat you" (Luke 6:27–28). It is releasing others from the debt of hurt they caused you so that your soul can be released from the prison of resentment.

And it restores you to the place of God's blessing. Ask Job.

Poor Job endured one of the worst single days any individual human has ever suffered through. Satan had received permission to swallow him in a tsunami of misery. On that one dreadful day, Job lost all ten of his children and everything associated with his business empire, his retirement holdings, and his career. Everything he had was gone. Soon after that, Job's health was taken from him as his body was covered in a rotting robe of agonizing boils. These awful events left his once blameless reputation in question and his heart broken.

Instead of encouragement, Job's friends offered words of rebuke and criticism, dumping guilt and shame on him.

Job became a captive in a prison of his own pain and God's silence. He spent what must have felt like an eternity shackled in torment and shame.

Then one day, God turned it around. Job was released from grievous pain into glorious prosperity.

God ended the captivity of Job. His boils disappeared, and his prosperity returned. He ended up with twice as many sheep, camels, oxen, and donkeys as he had owned before. He had seven more sons and three more daughters. He was a prisoner set free.

What was the key that turned the lock that opened the door of his jail cell? The answer is found in the last chapter of the Book of Job:

> The LORD turned the captivity of Job, when he prayed for his friends: also the LORD gave Job twice as much as he had before.
> JOB 42:10 KJV

Notice the six words, "*when he prayed for his friends.*" Job prayed the prayer of liberation. As he set his friends free and asked God to be merciful to them, God set him free.

The Lord had not been impressed with the self-righteous rebuke Job's friends brought this good man. In fact, their words put them in danger of judgment from the hand of God (see Job 42:7). But when Job prayed for them, God set Job free. When Job prayed for himself earlier, his misery was not removed. Almighty God seemed inactive and silent. But when Job prayed for the very ones who had hurt him and compounded his misery, God moved and set Job free!

There is great power in setting others free, for it releases God to liberate us and restore us to a place of blessing.

As We Forgive Our Debtors

Several years ago, I had a twenty-minute drive to work each day. I decided to use that time to pray through the Disciples Prayer as an outline (see Matthew 6:9–13). But on the first day, I found myself stuck on one phrase:

> *"And forgive us our debts, as we have forgiven our debtors [letting go of both the wrong and the resentment]."*
> MATTHEW 6:12 AMP

I had no problem confessing my sins and asking forgiveness. But I choked on the phrase "as we have forgiven our debtors." The images of three faces came to mind. My stomach knotted up and my pulse quickened. I had trusted, helped, and served with these three men for many years. But I was surprised and wounded when they handled a situation in a way that was very insensitive and extremely hurtful to my family and me.

I did not want to forgive them. I could never get back what they had taken from me. Plus, they had never showed remorse for their deeds.

The next day, I was again praying through the Lord's Prayer on my way to work.

Again, I came to the phrase "as we forgive our debtors."

Immediately the same three faces came to mind.

I certainly did not feel like forgiving them that day. But I knew I had no choice. I was aware that Jesus concluded the Lord's Prayer with a promise and a warning:

"For if you forgive men their trespasses, your heavenly Father will also forgive you. But if you do not forgive men their trespasses, neither will your Father forgive your trespasses."
MATTHEW 6:14–15 NKJV

So, by faith and not by feeling, I prayed the prayer of liberation for each one of these men:

Father, I was hurt by so and so because he did such and such. But by Your grace, I choose to forgive him today, to cancel the debt, and to free him of his offenses.

I wish I could say that the car was immediately filled with a mighty rushing wind and my heart immediately felt clean and fresh. But I felt nothing.

The same scene played out each day for the next couple of weeks. But as I chose to forgive the men who had hurt me and my family, their faces came to mind less vividly. Eventually they did not come to mind at all. I was free of them. . .I thought.

In the Sermon on the Mount, Jesus said, "Love your enemies, do good to those who hate you, bless those who curse you, pray for those who mistreat you" (Luke 6:27–28).

I sensed that to be fully free, the Lord wanted me to ask Him to bless the men who had hurt me so deeply.

Really? I thought. *Isn't it enough to just forgive them?*

Resentment can be a wicked vine with deep roots. Forgiveness, however, uproots the vine. Because of big hurts, the roots can remain deeply entrenched. Asking God to bless your enemies pulls out the roots of resentment.

By faith and not by feelings, I began to ask God to bless the three men who had wounded me.

About nine months later, I was in a setting where all three

of them were also in attendance. When I saw them, I felt no bit-terness, anger, or any other ugly emotions—just brotherly love. I looked each of them in the eye and gave them a sincere hug.

That truly was a miracle, the kind of miracle that can happen when we choose forgiveness and love, when we choose to bless and not curse those who have done us wrong.

Your Twenty-Eight Days to Powerful Prayer

1. Ask the Lord, "Who do I need to forgive?" As names and faces come to mind, do not argue or evaluate. Just write them down.
2. Start at the top of your list and begin to offer the prayer that liberates for each one.

Father, I was hurt by _____
because he/she/they did _____
and it made me feel _____,
But by the grace of God, I choose to forgive _____
_____ *today, to cancel the debt, and to free him/her/them of his/her/their offenses.*

Questions to Consider

1. Which story in this chapter resonated most deeply with you: Jesus forgiving His tormenters, Job forgiving his friends, the forgiven man who refused to forgive, or the story of the author forgiving his three friends?
2. What one truth from this chapter do you need to carry into your week?
3. Did you apply the forgiveness exercise at the end?

Notes

1. John MacArthur, *The MacArthur New Testament Commentary: Matthew 16–23* (Chicago: Moody Press, 1988), 148.
2. John Bevere, *The Bait of Satan* (Lake Mary, Florida: Charisma House, 1994), 135.

PRAYER BOOSTERS

Removing Roadblocks to Answered Prayer

You may have begun your twenty-eight days to powerful prayer and found yourself praying more than ever before. But what do you do when you don't see answers to those prayers? How do you handle it when you pray and pray yet nothing happens? What should you do when God does not answer the way you had hoped? Or how should you feel when He does not seem to answer at all?

I wasn't very far along in my Christian journey before I began to run into confusion about unanswered prayer. As I read more and more of the Bible, I began to see that there are many biblical reasons why God may not answer my prayers.

As we build our lives of prayer, we need to learn to recognize the roadblocks to answered prayers and to deal with them effectively.

Identifying the Roadblocks

What follows below is a list of nine roadblocks to answered prayer. Read through these carefully, and then ask yourself if one of them has been standing in your way to receiving what God has for you.

1. FAILING TO ASK

"Ask and it will be given to you; seek and you will find; knock and the door will be opened to you. . . . If you, then, though

you are evil, know how to give good gifts to your children, how
much more will your Father in heaven give good gifts to those
who ask him!"
MATTHEW 7:7, 11

God offers to give good gifts to His children, at least to those who ask Him. The book of James very specifically states, "You do not have because you do not ask God" (James 4:2).

The most obvious reason we fail to receive answers to prayer is that we fail to ask for them in the first place. God will certainly bless His children without our asking, but because He frequently commands us to ask, there are some blessings He withholds *until* we take the step of faith and ask Him (see Day 5).

2. IMPURE MOTIVES

When you ask, you do not receive, because you ask with wrong
motives, that you may spend what you get on your pleasures.
JAMES 4:3

God always has your best interests at heart. Therefore, don't be discouraged when He says "No" or "Wait" or when He gives you something other than what you asked for. Remember, *Father always knows best.*

Prayer is not dictation. Prayer is not us telling God what *we* want Him to do. Prayer is cooperating with God so that He can accomplish what *He* wants to do. Our motive for asking must be better than our own selfish desires.

One of God's goals for your Christian life is to help you become more like Jesus, who was selfless in every way (Philippians 2:3–7). God wants to help you become selfless too, and that's why He won't cater to your selfishness by answering your selfish prayer requests.

This, however, does not mean that God won't hear us when we pray for ourselves. God answered "Yes" when Abraham's servant asked for success in finding a bride for Isaac (Genesis 24), when Hannah asked God to remember her and bless her with a baby (1 Samuel 1), when David asked for forgiveness (2 Samuel 12), and when Solomon asked for wisdom (2 Chronicles 1). He answered "Yes" when Elijah asked for fire from heaven (1 Kings 18), when Hezekiah asked for deliverance (2 Kings 19), and when Nehemiah asked for favor from his boss (Nehemiah 1) and strength to complete his work (Nehemiah 6). These people's motives were pure, so their heavenly Father was pleased to give them good gifts.

3. PRAYING TO ATTRACT ATTENTION

"When you pray, don't be like the hypocrites who love to
pray publicly on street corners and in the synagogues
where everyone can see them. I tell you the truth,
that is all the reward they will ever get."
MATTHEW 6:5 NLT

Our lives are to be lived for an audience of one—the Lord. The person whose glory we are most interested in should be His not ours. If we pray merely to impress someone other than God, He won't answer us.

4. ASKING FOR SOMETHING OUTSIDE GOD'S WILL

This is the confidence we have in approaching God: that if
we ask anything according to his will, he hears us. And if
we know that he hears us—whatever we ask—we know
that we have what we asked of him.
1 JOHN 5:14–15

Since God answers our prayers "if we ask. . .according to His will," then we can assume that He does not respond if we ask for something outside of His will. Our requests need to align with His purpose and plan.

We know that God's will does not contradict God's Word. Therefore, God's will won't give you something He forbids in scripture. God is a good Father. If what we ask for could be detrimental to us or to others, He won't honor our requests.

Conversely, when we ask for those things that lead to the good of others, that develops our godliness, and that enhances His glory, God will probably say "Yes."

5. UNRESOLVED SIN

> *If I had not confessed the sin in my heart, the Lord would not have listened.*
> PSALM 66:18 NLT

> *Indeed, the LORD's hand is not too short to save, and His ear is not too deaf to hear. But your iniquities have built barriers between you and your God, and your sins have made Him hide His face from you so that He does not listen.*
> ISAIAH 59:1–2 HCSB

Because God is so merciful and gracious, He will occasionally answer some of our prayers even though we still have areas of sin in our lives. But when we fail to confess our sin, He is far less likely to answer. When we have known sin in our lives, the prayer God waits to answer is a prayer of confession for our sins (see Day 10).

Once our hearts are clean and our conscience is clear, we can have great confidence that God will hear and answer our prayers:

> *Dear friends, if our conscience doesn't condemn us, we have confidence before God and can receive whatever we ask from Him because we keep His commands and do what is pleasing in His sight.*
> 1 JOHN 3:21–22 HCSB

6. IGNORING GOD

> *The LORD is far from the wicked, but he hears the prayer of the righteous.*
> PROVERBS 15:29

> *If anyone turns a deaf ear to my instruction, even their prayers are detestable.*
> PROVERBS 28:9

"The eyes of the LORD watch over those who do right, and his ears are open to their prayers. But the LORD turns his face against those who do evil."
1 PETER 3:12 NLT

It is simple: When we ignore God, He ignores us. But if we listen to God, obey His instruction, try to do the right thing, and run from wickedness, He hears and answers our prayers.

7. NEGLECTING THE POOR

Whoever shuts their ears to the cry of the poor will also cry out and not be answered.
PROVERBS 21:13

The way we respond to the cries of the poor can impact the way God responds to our own cries. God loves the poor (Psalm 10:14; Psalm 140:12; Isaiah 25:4) and blesses those who actively care for them (Proverbs 22:9; Deuteronomy 15:10; Luke 14:12–14). But God curses those who don't (Isaiah 10:1–3; Ezekiel 16:49). He expects us to care for the poor (1 John 3:17; Galatians 2:9–10).

God equates how we treat the poor with how we feel about Him:

Whoever oppresses the poor shows contempt for their Maker, but whoever is kind to the needy honors God.
PROVERBS 14:31

Whoever is kind to the poor lends to the LORD, and he will reward them for what they have done.
PROVERBS 19:17

"And the King will answer them, 'I assure you: Whatever you did for one of the least of these brothers of Mine, you did for Me.'"
MATTHEW 25:40 HCSB

"Then He will answer them, 'I assure you: Whatever you did not do for one of the least of these, you did not do for Me either.'"
MATTHEW 25:45 HCSB

For years, I neglected the poor, yet God still heard and answered many of my prayers. But through starting a church in the inner city of Las Vegas, I developed a heart for the poor and became active in consistently serving them. I have been enriched in the process, and I believe my service has made it more likely that the Lord will answer my prayers.

8. NEGLECTING GOD'S WORD

"If you remain in me and my words remain in you, ask whatever you wish, and it will be done for you."
JOHN 15:7

God equates our attitude toward His Word with our attitude toward Him. Filling our lives with His Word and obeying it directs our prayers and enables us to get what we ask for. On the other hand, neglecting His Word will limit the answers we receive.

9. DISHONORING YOUR SPOUSE

Wives, in the same way submit yourselves to your own husbands so that, if any of them do notbelieve the word, they may be won over without words by the behavior of their wives.
1 PETER 3:1 NIV

Likewise, ye husbands, dwell with them according to knowledge, giving honour unto the wife, as unto the weaker vessel, and as being heirs together of the grace of life; that your prayers be not hindered.
1 PETER 3:7 KJV

Marriage should create the ultimate prayer partnership. But when one or both of the mates neglect to fulfill God's roles for marriage and thereby dishonors the other spouse, it will negatively impact their prayers.

Your Twenty-Eight Days to Powerful Prayer

I believe it's a good idea to periodically work through the above roadblocks to make sure that you have done your part to deal with the possible reasons for unanswered prayer. If God has alerted you to some of the above-mentioned roadblocks, agree with Him, confess the sin, and ask Him to help you make the necessary changes.

The apostle John encourages us to do just that in these verses:

> *If we claim to be without sin, we deceive ourselves*
> *and the truth is not in us. If we confess our sins,*
> *he is faithful and just and will forgive us our sins*
> *and purify us from all unrighteousness.*
> 1 JOHN 1:8–9

Questions to Consider

1. Have you ever gone through a time when it seemed that God wasn't answering your prayers?
2. Which of the nine roadblocks could possibly be hindering your prayers?
3. Will you choose to agree with God, confess the sin, and ask Him to help you make the necessary changes?

PRAYER BOOSTERS

Humility in Prayer

Do you really believe that God listens to your prayer? Is He drawn to you and your need or is He repelled?

What type of attitudes do you think attract God's attention? What heart condition lends fuel to the effectiveness of your prayers?

Jesus told a story that addressed these very questions.

Two Men, Two Prayers

Jesus once told some important Jewish leaders a story about prayer. He wanted them to understand that external religion means nothing and an inner relationship with God means everything. He made the point that self-righteousness is no substitute for the true righteousness that can only be received as a gift from God.

Here's how Jesus' story started:

> *To some who were confident of their own righteousness and looked down on everyone else, Jesus told this parable: "Two men went up to the temple to pray, one a Pharisee and the other a tax collector."*
> Luke 18:9–10

Jesus' audience would know that the two men in the story were representative of the two extremes in their religious hierarchy. The Pharisees were highly religious and, therefore, highly esteemed. They were so intent on achieving external holiness that they added about a thousand rules to the more than six hundred rules already found in the Old Testament.

The Jews of Jesus' time scorned the tax collectors. Tax collectors not only worked for the Roman government, but they also collected unjust taxes from their own people, the Jews.

In the mind of a first-century Jew, God must certainly love the Pharisees and hate the tax collectors. But what do you think? If you needed someone to teach you to pray, which would you select—the religious Pharisee or the wicked tax collector? Jesus' story shows that the answer to that question isn't what many might think:

> *"The Pharisee stood by himself and prayed: 'God, I thank you that I am not like other people—robbers, evildoers, adulterers—or even like this tax collector. I fast twice a week and give a tenth of all I get.'"*
> LUKE 18:11–12

This Pharisee was morally exemplary. He was faithful to his wife, honest in his dealings, and upright with his finances. If that wasn't impressive enough, he had outstanding religious habits, fasting two days a week and giving 10 percent of his income in offerings. What a guy! And he knew it.

Now, about that other guy:

> *"But the tax collector stood at a distance. He would not even look up to heaven, but beat his breast and said, 'God, have mercy on me, a sinner.'"*
> LUKE 18:13

Unlike the Pharisee, when the tax collector prayed, he slumped back in the shadows. Unlike the Pharisee, he did not even try to compare himself with others. He knew he was a sinner, and all he could do was cry out to God for mercy.

What did Jesus think of his prayer?

"I tell you that this man, rather than the other, went home justified before God. For all those who exalt themselves will be humbled, and those who humble themselves will be exalted."
LUKE 18:14

Jesus clearly stated that the humble, utterly-dependent-upon-God tax collector was the one who impressed Him. The point of the story is that one of the essential keys to effective prayer is a dependent, humble heart.

This is a consistent theme throughout scripture:

1. HUMILITY: ESSENTIAL FOR ANSWERED PRAYER

He does not forget the cry of the humble.
PSALM 9:12 NKJV

If my people, who are called by my name, will humble themselves and pray and seek my face and turn from their wicked ways, then I will hear from heaven, and I will forgive their sin and will heal their land.
2 CHRONICLES 7:14

2. HUMILITY: ESSENTIAL TO A STRONG, GROWING, VICTORIOUS LIFE

He crowns the humble with victory.
PSALM 149:4

He guides the humble in what is right and teaches them his way.
PSALM 25:9

The LORD sustains the humble but casts the wicked to the ground.
PSALM 147:6

3. HUMILITY: THE DOORWAY TO GOD'S FAVOR AND HONOR

He mocks proud mockers but shows favor to the humble and oppressed.
PROVERBS 3:34

When pride comes, then comes disgrace,
but with humility comes wisdom.
PROVERBS 11:2

Pride brings a person low, but the lowly in spirit gain honor.
PROVERBS 29:23

All of you, clothe yourselves with humility toward
one another, because, "God opposes the proud
but shows favor to the humble."
1 PETER 5:5

"God opposes the proud but shows favor to the humble."
JAMES 4:6

4. HUMILITY: A CONDITION FOR REVIVAL

For this is what the high and exalted One says—he who lives
forever, whose name is holy: "I live in a high and holy place, but
also with the one who is contrite and lowly in spirit, to revive
the spirit of the lowly and to revive the heart of the contrite."
ISAIAH 57:15

"I am about to spit you out of my mouth. You say, 'I am rich; I
have acquired wealth and do not need a thing.' But you do not
realize that you are wretched, pitiful, poor, blind and naked."
REVELATION 3:16–17

5. JESUS: THE PERFECT EXAMPLE OF HUMILITY

Have the same mindset as Christ Jesus: Who, being in very
nature God, did not consider equality with God something to
be used to his own advantage; rather, he made himself nothing
by taking the very nature of a servant, being made in human
likeness. And being found in appearance as a man, he humbled
himself by becoming obedient to death—even death on a cross!
PHILIPPIANS 2:5–8

Therefore God exalted him to the highest place and gave him the name that is above every name, that at the name of Jesus every knee should bow, in heaven and on earth and under the earth, and every tongue acknowledge that Jesus Christ is Lord, to the glory of God the Father.
PHILIPPIANS 2:9–11

He Forgot the Secret of His Success

Saul was a shy, humble, young man who spent his life avoiding the spotlight. At the age of thirty, the Lord suddenly plucked him from obscurity, transformed his personality, and made him the first king of Israel.

Unfortunately, Saul forgot where he came from and who he was without the Lord. That led to his downfall.

One time, a huge Philistine army attacked Saul and his army of three thousand men (1 Samuel 13:1–7). Pressure has a way of revealing a person's true character, and the revelation was an ugly one for Saul.

King Saul knew he needed God's help, but he was impatient for the priest Samuel to come and secure it through burnt offerings. When he saw his small army abandoning him and the enemy bearing down on him, he went ahead of God, disobeyed the Lord's teaching, and arrogantly acted as though he was Israel's high priest (1 Samuel 13:8–9).

Later, instead of humbling himself and admitting his sin, King Saul haughtily tried to justify his disobedience. But God was looking for a man He could fully trust (1 Samuel 13:10–14), and because of Saul's cavalier disregard for God's words, He took His presence from Saul—as well as the blessing accompanying it.

That was tragic enough. But it got much worse for Saul.

God gave King Saul and his army a great victory over the Amalekites. But Saul again failed to fully obey Him. Instead of humbly honoring God for the victory, he arrogantly built a monument to himself (1 Samuel 15:1–12).

When Saul saw the prophet Samuel coming, he immediately began bragging about having fully obeyed the Lord's instructions. But Samuel knew better and confronted Saul over his disobedience. Samuel told Saul that God was grieved over how the king, once a humble man—"You were once small in your own eyes" (1 Samuel 15:17)—had forgotten who he was and how desperately he needed God. Finally, Samuel gave Saul a crushing pronouncement of warning and judgment:

> "Does the LORD delight in burnt offerings and sacrifices
> as much as in obeying the LORD? To obey is better than
> sacrifice, and to heed is better than the fat of rams.
> For rebellion is like the sin of divination, and arrogance
> like the evil of idolatry. Because you have rejected
> the word of the LORD, he has rejected you as king."
> 1 SAMUEL 15:22–23

Notice the phrase: "arrogance [is] like the evil of idolatry." Why? In a sense, arrogance is idolatry because it means worshiping self instead of the Lord.

It's important that we never minimize the importance of humility in pleasing God and enhancing effectiveness in prayer. God does not measure prayer merely by the words said. He looks at the heart from which those words spring.

Your Twenty-Eight Days to Powerful Prayer

God is drawn to the humble and repulsed by the arrogant. Which are you? Are you a person who attracts God's presence or repels it? How you come down on the matter of pride or humility provides the answer to those questions.

The checklist below, when taken honestly, reveals areas where proud, self-centeredness becomes a God-repellent. Honestly answer each question of the checklist. Circle each question in which the honest answer is "yes." Where necessary, ask God for forgiveness.

Do you:

- Think primarily about yourself when you make decisions?
- Feel as though you must have your own way?

- Look down on others?
- Feel the need to prove yourself?
- Focus on others' mistakes?
- Think first about your rights?
- Desire to be served?
- Feel driven to be recognized and appreciated?
- Feel wounded when others are recognized and you are not?
- Think God is privileged to have your service?
- Get defensive when criticized?
- Work to maintain your image and reputation?
- Find it difficult to say "I'm sorry"?
- Justify your mistakes and excuse your sin?
- Regret sin only when you get caught or suffer the consequences?
- Quickly blame others?
- Keep people at a safe distance?
- Use or manipulate people?
- Expect others to take the first step of reconciliation?
- Constantly compare and compete with others?
- Live as though you are self-sufficient?
- Disobey God when His will goes against what you want?

Questions to Consider

1. What does it mean to be humble in prayer?
2. How did you do on the twenty-two-question test for pride in this chapter? How many times did you have to honestly answer "Yes"?
3. How can you humble yourself before God every day?
4. Why do you think God wants us to be humble and not prideful?

PRAYER BOOSTERS

Persistence in Prayer

What do you do when you sincerely pray for something. . .and nothing happens? Do you get discouraged. . .or even just stop praying about the matter?

This chapter, especially the story of the persistent widow, will show you that maybe you should continue praying, *especially* when God seems slow to answer.

A Picture of Persistence

I don't fully understand why, but God has designed prayer so that it involves an aspect of persistence. Jesus wanted us to appreciate the need for perseverance in prayer, so He told the following story to encourage us to continue praying about something until that something happens:

> Now Jesus was telling the disciples a parable to make the point that at all times they ought to pray and not give up and lose heart, saying, "In a certain city there was a judge who did not fear God and had no respect for man. There was a [desperate] widow in that city and she kept coming to him and saying, 'Give me justice and legal protection from my adversary.' For a time he would not; but later he said to himself, 'Even though I do not fear God nor respect man, yet because this widow continues to bother me, I will give her justice and legal protection; otherwise by continually coming she [will be an intolerable annoyance and she] will wear me out.'" Then the Lord said,

"Listen to what the unjust judge says! And will not [our just] God defend and avenge His elect [His chosen ones] who cry out to Him day and night? Will He delay [in providing justice] on their behalf? I tell you that He will defend and avenge them quickly. However, when the Son of Man comes, will He find [this kind of persistent] faith on the earth?"
LUKE 18:1–8 AMP

When we desperately need something from God, He wants us to keep praying about it and not give up (verse 1). In the above story, the widow kept coming to the judge day after day (verse 3), but the wicked judge was not inclined to help her (verse 4). Eventually, however, he decided to help her *because* her "continual coming" was going to "wear him out" (verse 5).

Jesus told His followers to learn from the words of this unjust judge (verse 6). Our God will defend and avenge us when we "cry out to Him day and night" (verse 7), so displaying persistence in prayer is an important expression of faith (verse 8).

God grows our faith and honors it when we persist in prayer.

The Relentless Mother

One day, a non-Jewish woman approached Jesus and asked for help with her demon-possessed daughter (Matthew 15:22). However, because she was not Jewish, He was initially reluctant to respond. But this woman stubbornly refused to take no for an answer. She kept seeking His help until He finally relented:

Then Jesus said to her, "Woman, you have great faith! Your request is granted." And her daughter was healed at that moment.
MATTHEW 15:28

This desperate woman's need and her faith would not allow her to quit. And she got her answer. God responded to her relentless faith.

He responds to our relentless faith as well.

The Persevering Prophet

Elijah is one of my favorite prophets. We don't know much about him, but we do know that he had an amazing commitment to prayer. Elijah prayed and caused the rain to completely stop . . .for three years (1 Kings 17:1; James 5:16–17). He also single-handedly took on the wicked, murderous King Ahab and Queen Jezebel and their four hundred evil prophets in a duel between their god and the true God. Then he boldly called down fire from heaven, crushing the opposition and helping point the nation of Israel back to the Lord (1 Kings 18:16–39). Wow!

But one time, Elijah did not get answers so quickly and easily. After winning the showdown with Ahab's pagan god, he told the evil king that it was going to rain again. Then he climbed a mountain to pray. He instructed his servant to search the sky as he prayed.

But there were no clouds.

He continued to pray.

Still no clouds.

Seven times he prayed. Seven times he sent his servant back to search.

Finally, "The seventh time the servant reported, 'A cloud as small as a man's hand is rising from the sea'" (1 Kings 18:44). Then it happened: "The sky grew black with clouds, the wind rose, a heavy rain started falling" (1 Kings 18:45).

Even powerhouse prophets sometimes have to persist in prayer!

The Determined Intercessor

Abraham is known as the father of our faith. One day, the Lord alerted Abraham that He was about to destroy the city of Sodom because of its extreme wickedness. Abraham responded by interceding for Sodom, asking God to spare the city if there were at least fifty righteous people living there. God agreed to his request (Genesis 18:16–26).

But Abraham was determined. He begged God to spare

Sodom if forty-five righteous people lived there. God agreed (Genesis 18:27–28).

Then Abraham asked for mercy on Sodom on behalf of forty righteous persons. Again, he succeeded (Genesis 18:29).

Abraham then pleaded with the Lord to spare Sodom if thirty righteous persons lived there. God said yes (Genesis 18:30).

Abraham was not finished. He cried out to God to respond with mercy if there were only twenty righteous ones. Again, God agreed (Genesis 18:31).

Confident that there had to be ten righteous persons in the city, Abraham made his sixth and final appeal to God to save the city if just ten righteous ones lived there. Again, the Lord said He would not destroy the city if there were indeed ten righteous people in Sodom (Genesis 18:32).

Abraham approached God on behalf of Sodom six times. His determined persistence in intercession potentially altered the plans of the Lord God on behalf of an entire city. One man's relentless prayers had potentially spared the lives of many people.

Unfortunately, Abraham was overly optimistic. There weren't ten righteous ones in Sodom. But perhaps he quit too soon. He should have persisted longer, asking God to spare the city on behalf of just a few people.

The Tenacious Prophet

As we will discuss in Day 22, prayer may spark spiritual warfare. That was the case with the great prophet-statesman Daniel when he fasted and prayed for three weeks and saw no response. Even though the Lord had sent the answer the moment Daniel began to pray, it took three more weeks of prayer, and warfare by Gabriel, before Daniel's answer arrived (Daniel 10:12–13). It took persistence for the answer to come.

The Persistence of George Mueller

George Mueller is known for having recorded fifty thousand answered prayers in his journal. One of the aspects of Mueller's remarkable prayer life was his practice of persisting in petition-ing God until he received an answer.

Mueller testified that at one point in his life, he had received thirty thousand definite answers to prayer on the *first day* of ask-ing. But when it came to the especially big and/or difficult re-quests, he believed that the bigger the request, the greater the number of prayers required to secure it. He felt that he should show his trust in God by asking two, three, four times a day until the breakthrough came.

On one occasion, Mueller's orphanages desperately needed more workers. His response was to lead his staff to triple their daily group prayer times until God supplied the needed staff.

On another occasion, Mueller and his staff needed a huge amount of money to double his ministry's space to house more orphans. His plan was to increase the amount of prayer about the need. During this time, he wrote,

> *Many and great may be the difficulties. Thousands and thou-sands of prayers may have to ascend to God before the full answer is obtained.*[1]

God responded. Money poured in from all over the world. When the last of the donations arrived, Mueller gave thanks saying,

> *Thousands of times I have asked the Lord for the means to build these two homes and now I have to the full received the answer.*[2]

Mueller is known for having prayed for five young men to be saved. After daily prayer year after year, they all eventually came to Christ. In fact, the last two were converted only after fifty-two years of daily, disciplined, devoted prayer.

Your Twenty-Eight Days to Powerful Prayer

The great evangelist D. L. Moody appreciated the need for per-sistence in petitioning. He wrote, "Some people think God does not like to be troubled with our constant coming and asking. The only way to trouble God is not to come at all. He encourages us to come to Him repeatedly and press our claims."[3]

In George Mueller's autobiography, we read his formula for prevailing prayer: "It is not enough to begin to pray, nor to pray aright; nor is it enough to continue for a time to pray; but we must patiently, believing, continue in prayer until we obtain an answer."[4]

I suggest that you make a list of three to seven big things you deeply need and want and that God would be glorified by giving to you. They should be things you can ask for with full confidence. They could relate to your financial situation, your health, your relationships, a family member, a friend, your job, your ministry, or your future. List them below.

1.
2.
3.
4.
5.
6.
7.

Make a commitment to pray every day (or several times a day) until the answer comes or until God tells you to stop. As you pray for these things day after day, the Lord will probably refine your request. Keep praying until He responds.

Questions to Consider

1. Which of the six examples of persistent prayer given in this chapter did you find most interesting or inspiring? Why?
2. What excites you the most in this chapter?
3. When have you persisted in prayer and seen God answer?

Notes

1. George Mueller, quoted by Basil Miller, *George Mueller: Man of Faith and Miracles* (Men of Faith) (Minneapolis, Minnesota: Bethany House Publishers, reprinted edition 1972), 79.
2. Ibid.
3. D. L. Moody, *Prevailing Prayer* (Chicago: Moody Press, 1970), 91–92.
4. George Mueller, quoted by Wesley L. Duewel, *Mighty Prevailing Prayer* (Grand Rapids, Michigan: Zondervan), Kindle Edition, 149.

PRAYER BOOSTERS

Faith in Prayer

I was in Brazil for two weeks of teaching and preaching. One Saturday, my hosts took me for lunch at a wonderful Brazilian churrasco steak house. Near the end of our meal, a handsome young waiter asked us if we were pastors and where we went to church. He told us he had overheard us talking and felt he needed to go to church. One of our hosts invited him to come hear me speak the next day.

As we discussed the interest our waiter had expressed in coming to church, I suddenly had a very clear thought: *If he comes to church tomorrow, he will be saved.* We prayed for him that day, and I was able to pray a simple prayer of confident faith and gratitude for what I knew was his pending salvation.

I spoke twice that afternoon, and the next day, Sunday, I was about to give my fourth sermon of the day. As the service began, one of my hosts brought the young waiter and his pretty wife and baby to meet me. As they returned to their seats, I told the pastor standing next to me, "God is working. That young man is going to get saved tonight."

Even though the message was more about how to do evangelism than how to be saved, at the end of my talk, I gave an appeal for people to come to Christ. Three men and a lady responded.

I was going to move on, but I felt the Holy Spirit prompt me to give the invitation one more time. When I did, a teenager and her mother, as well as a young man, came to the front asking to be saved. Then I saw the waiter and his wife beginning to cry as they sat in the back row. They stepped into the aisle, walked all the way to the front, and stood in front of me, broken and weeping.

I led all the respondents in a prayer. Then the church's pastors dealt with each one individually. The worship band led a song, and the senior pastor closed the service. Afterward, one of the pastors brought the young couple to me. Their tears were replaced with giant smiles of joy. I had no doubt that they had been saved, and I had no doubt that prayer and faith had played a role.

How Faith Makes a Difference

Does faith make a difference in whether or not God answers my prayers? According to the Bible, the answer is "Yes." The Bible repeatedly stresses the importance of faith in powerful prayer.

1. Faith plays an important role in God's work on earth. Nothing caused Jesus greater disappointment than the lack of faith in His followers. Five times He exclaimed, "You of little faith" (Matthew 6:30; 8:36; 14:31; 16:8; Luke 12:28). He also asked, "Do you still have no faith?" (Mark 4:40) and "Where is your faith?" (Luke 8:25).

Three more times Jesus made faith a condition for God doing mighty works, saying, "If you have faith" (Matthew 17:20; 21:21; Luke 17:6). He also said, "Because you have so little faith" (Matthew 17:20); "Stop doubting and believe" (John 20:27); "Rise and go; your faith has made you well" (Luke 7:19); and "Your faith has healed you" (Mark 5:34; 10:52).

The most telling comment in the Gospels about the role of faith in miracles involves Jesus' return trip to His hometown of Nazareth: "He did not do many miracles there because of their lack of faith" (Matthew 13:58). The lack of faith among the people in Jesus' hometown limited Him in what He would do there. Regarding this lack of faith, Wesley Duewel stated,

> It is absolutely clear that our lack of faith limits God's freedom of working mightily. It stopped Jesus from using His

miracle-working power (Mark 6:5). *From the standpoint of omnipotence, God is almighty—His power is utterly unlimited. From the standpoint of His sovereignty, God can do what He will. But from the standpoint of His grace, He has chosen normally to limit His miracle answers to our believing. "According to your faith" (Matthew 9:29), said Jesus.*[1]

2. Faith may be required to receive answers to prayer. Pastor James, who wrote a book of the New Testament, said that God loves to give us wisdom when we ask for it, but that we can't go back and forth between faith and doubt. We need to ask with faith:

> *If any of you lacks wisdom, you should ask God, who gives generously to all without finding fault, and it will be given to you. But when you ask, you must believe and not doubt, because the one who doubts is like a wave of the sea, blown and tossed by the wind. That person should not expect to receive anything from the Lord.*
> JAMES 1:5–8

Jesus said that faith-filled prayer can move mountains and leads to answered prayer:

> *"Have faith in God," Jesus answered. "Truly I tell you, if anyone says to this mountain, 'Go, throw yourself into the sea,' and does not doubt in their heart but believes that what they say will happen, it will be done for them. Therefore I tell you, whatever you ask for in prayer, believe that you have received it, and it will be yours."*
> MARK 11:22–24

Six Keys to Having Bold Faith in Prayer

If you agree that faith is essential to power in prayer (and you should), the question remains, "How can I pray with bold faith?" Here are six keys to having bold faith when you pray:

1. Align your requests with the will of God. The apostle John, who heard Jesus' teaching on faith in person, wrote this about one of the keys to praying in faith, namely knowing that you are praying according to God's will:

> This is the confidence we have in approaching God: that if we ask anything according to his will, he hears us. And if we know that he hears us—whatever we ask—we know that we have what we asked of him.
> 1 JOHN 5:14–15

J. O. Sanders writes, "If faith is the gift of God, and it is, He will not give it to someone in order to encourage the person to do something contrary to His will."[2]

2. Base your requests on the promise or promises of God. Charles Spurgeon was one of the greatest preachers who ever lived. He was known for fearlessly claiming God's promises and quoting them back to Him. In his book *God's Checkbook: Daily Drawing on God's Treasury*, Spurgeon explains,

> A promise from God may very instructively be compared to a check payable to order. It is given to the believer with the view of bestowing upon him some good thing. It is not meant that he should read it over comfortably and have done with it. No, he is to treat it as a reality as a man treats a check.[3]

Spurgeon continues, "He must believingly *present* the promise to the Lord, as a man presents a check at the counter of the bank. He must plead it by prayer, expecting to have it fulfilled."[4] (Italics are Spurgeon's.)

3. Look for confirmation. Wesley Deuwel advises the prayer warrior to recognize that if a promise is God's promise to you at a given time, He will not only deeply impress it upon your heart, He will also provide confirming indicators. These indicators may include circumstances, the words of others, or a strong sense of peace.[5]

4. Recognize a prayer burden. When God gives us a burden for something, He also calls us to pray with confidence, knowing that He wants to work. Oswald Sanders tells of a missionary couple who many years ago was struggling to make progress with the people in Three Clan Village in China. Then something inexplicably changed. Spiritual breakthroughs began to happen throughout the village as relationships were mended. The missionaries did not realize it, but a letter giving the explanation was on the way. Two months later, the letter arrived. It said,

> I must write and tell you what happened today. All morning I could not do my housework because of the burden on me concerning Three Clan Village. So finally, I went to the telephone and called Mrs. W. She said she had been feeling the same way and suggested we call Mrs. J. and all go to prayer together. We did so, each in her own kitchen. We spent the morning in intercession for three quarrelling clans. We feel God has answered.

The date on the letter corresponded exactly with the victory gained in Three Clan Village.[6]

5. Focus on God's faithfulness, not your faithlessness. I often feel like the father of the epileptic boy who prayed, "I do believe; help me overcome my unbelief!" (Mark 9:24). My faith is often imperfect, fickle, and tainted with unbelief. But God is faithful to keep His promises. When we focus on Him, faith follows. The closer we draw to Him, the purer and stronger our faith becomes.

6. Express your faith with words of thanksgiving. Lazarus was dead and had been lying in a tomb for several days. But Jesus offered a simple, yet powerful prayer of faith for him:

> "Father, I thank you that you have heard me. I knew that you always hear me, but I said this for the benefit of the people

standing here, that they may believe that you sent me." When he had said this, Jesus called in a loud voice, "Lazarus, come out!" The dead man came out.
JOHN 11:41-44

Notice that Jesus did not make a request when He prayed but instead offered a prayer of gratitude for what God was about to do. I find that when my prayers lack faith, I can change that by shifting my requests from asking God to work to thanking Him because He is working.

Your Twenty-Eight Days to Powerful Prayer

I encourage you to take your prayer life to a new level by learning to transact business with God by praying in faith. Make the effort to be specific, bold, and confident as you come to God in your prayers today.

Questions to Consider

1. How would you rate your prayers? Are they weak and wimpy or strong and mighty?
2. What are two things that jumped out at you from this chapter? Why?
3. How can you better apply faith to your prayer life every day?

Notes

1. Wesley L. Duewel, *Mighty Prevailing Prayer* (Grand Rapids, Michigan: Zondervan) Kindle Edition, 92-93.
2. J. Oswald Sanders, *Prayer Power Unlimited* (Grand Rapids, Michigan: Discovery House Publishers), Kindle Edition.
3. Charles Spurgeon, *God's Checkbook: Daily Drawing on God's Treasury* (Chicago: Moody Press, n.d.), ii.
4. Ibid.
5. Wesley Duewel, *Touch the World Through Prayer* (Grand Rapids, Michigan: Zondervan, 1986), 147.
6. Sanders.

PRAYER BOOSTERS

Unity in Prayer

Would you like to add to your prayer life a principle that will guide you to the Lord's will in your prayers? Do you often need encouragement to persevere in your prayers? Do you want to add multiplied power to your prayers? Do you have a significant need and need a significant answer?

If you answered any of those questions "Yes," I suggest that you apply the principle of united prayer.

United prayer is two or more believers praying together in agreement about the same thing or things. It is partnering with the Lord Jesus in His intercessions for others. It is tapping into the promised power of prayer partnership.

Why Unity in Prayer?

What follows is five reasons why unity in prayer is important:

1. The Lord blesses spiritual unity. King David observed the blessings of unity when he wrote:

> *How good and pleasant it is when God's people live together in unity!. . . For there the LORD bestows his blessing.*
> PSALM 133:1, 3

2. Spiritual partnership brings greater accomplishment, increased encouragement, and added protection. King Solomon, David's son, also observed the benefits of unity and partnership:
> *Two are better than one, because they have a good return for*

their labor: If either of them falls down, one can help the other up. But pity anyone who falls and has no one to help them up. . . . Though one may be overpowered, two can defend themselves. A cord of three strands is not quickly broken.
ECCLESIASTES 4:9–10, 12

3. There can be exponential power in spiritual partnership. Moses spoke on more than one occasion of the exponential power of partnership. He mentioned that "Five of you will chase a hundred, and a hundred of you will chase ten thousand, and your enemies will fall by the sword before you" (Leviticus 26:8), and "one man can chase a thousand but two can put ten thousand to flight" (Deuteronomy 32:30).

Regarding these verses, Charles Spurgeon said, "There is accumulated power in united intercession; two do not only double the force, but multiply it tenfold." He then added, "God grant to each of us a praying partner."[1]

4. Spiritual unity was the primary prayer request Jesus made for His disciples. One of the primary themes of Jesus' final prayer in the Garden of Gethsemane was His plea for unity within His disciples:

"I pray for them. . . . Holy Father, protect them by the power of your name, the name you gave me, so that they may be one as we are one."
JOHN 17:9, 11

"My prayer is not for them alone. I pray also for those who will believe in me through their message, that all of them may be one. . .that they may be one as we are one—I in them and you in me—so that they may be brought to complete unity. Then the world will know that you sent me and have loved them even as you have loved me."
JOHN 17:20–23

5. Jesus promised increased answers and blessings from united prayer.

> *"Again, truly I tell you that if two of you on earth*
> *agree about anything they ask for, it will be done*
> *for them by my Father in heaven. For where two*
> *or three gather in my name, there am I with them."*
> MATTHEW 18:19–20

The word *agree* in this passage's original language is *symphoneo*—literally "sound together," from which we get our word *symphony*. A symphony is many instruments all playing the same song, all playing off the same score, and all playing the same measure at the same time. When the many and varied instruments of an orchestra all join in one harmony, we call it a symphony.

The goal in prayer is not for me to pray for my agenda and you to pray for yours. The goal is for both of us to lay down our wishes and ask God to fulfill His desires. The power of our agreement comes when we both agree with the Lord.

Agreement in prayer refers to a deep sense that a specific request is indeed the will of God and that God is stirring us to pray about it now because He desires to answer it soon.

Characteristics of the Prayer of Agreement

Here is a list of characteristics of the prayer of agreement:

- The request agrees and aligns with God's Word.
- The request expresses God's will.
- The Holy Spirit confirms the request to each person.
- The request has a spiritual sense of compulsion to bring it to God and urgency that He is desiring to act.

Jesus made a bold promise: if we are confident that our request aligns with God's Word and expresses His will, and if we have sensed both the confirmation of the Spirit and the awareness that the timing is right, then we can count on God to answer our rain all day Saturday and Sunday. Rain would ruin our "church in the park" idea. Even if it rained only on Saturday, the water would not be drained from the park by Sunday.

It poured all day Saturday. Several of us met in the park and stood in the rain praying for the rain to stop and the wind to come out to dry the grass. We agreed together not only that the Lord was able to stop the rain, but that He *would*. "Stop the rain!" we cried out to God. "Send wind to dry the grass."

However, it continued to rain all afternoon and into the evening.

Jesus promised that united prayer brings big results, so we continued praying.

Late that night the rain stopped. A strong wind blew through the valley, drying up the grass in the park. On Sunday morning the sun was shining. We held church in the park and seven people were saved! Then we enjoyed a great party in the park afterwards.[2]

The Book of Acts: A Story of the Power of United Prayer

After Jesus ascended back into heaven, the apostles called a prayer meeting. For the next week, they met by the temple "continually united in prayer" and cried out to God for an outpouring of the Holy Spirit (Acts 1:14 HCSB). As a result, God sent the Holy Spirit, the church was born, and three thousand people were saved and baptized (Acts 2:1–41).

The united prayer meeting *preceded* the huge evangelistic harvest. United prayer was the first thing on their agenda. Pentecost was preceded by a prayer meeting.

Soon after that, the first church was growing. This "new" movement also had a very public major healing on its record (Acts 3:1–10). The Jewish authorities felt threatened, and they arrested Peter and John and dragged them before the high priest and other top leaders to question their authority to heal. Peter took the opportunity to preach Jesus to them. Because the healing was undeniable, the only thing the authorities could do united, agreed-upon requests. Instead of begging Him to act, we can thank Him in advance for answering.

"Gone"

I regularly pray for people to be physically healed, but I do not often see them immediately receive the healing I asked for. But one night in a wonderful corporate gathering of prayer and worship, a young lady, filled with fear, asked us to pray about a cancerous tumor on her breast. Several of us sensed that it was God's desire to heal her, and together we cried out to God for her healing.

Then we sent her to the restroom to check the lump. She came back and told us, "It is definitely smaller, but it is still there."

Again, we cried out to God for her complete healing.

She went into the restroom again and came out beaming. "Gone!" she said. "The lump is gone!"

When she went to the doctor, an exam confirmed what she had said. The lump was completely gone. She was healed!

We believed that God healed this woman because we were united in the belief that He wanted to heal her—and we prayed in accordance with that belief.

"Stop the Rain"

When we started a church in Las Vegas, we met for Sunday worship at a public school building. One Friday afternoon a secretary from the school board called to tell us we could not meet in the school that weekend.

What would we do?

We "just happened" to be in the midst of a special prayer emphasis involving twenty-one corporate prayer meetings in twenty-one days. After we prayed, the Lord gave us a Plan B.

We felt God direct us to hold our Sunday church service in the park near the school. Immediately after the service, we would have a Park Party with inflatables, grills, and game One problem, though. The weather services all predicted co was try to intimidate Peter and John into not talking about Jesus. That did not work.

Peter and John returned to the church and reported what had occurred. The response of the Christians was a big, beautiful, united prayer meeting. Instead of asking for protection, they asked for God to give them greater boldness to speak God's Word:

> When they heard this, they raised their voices together in prayer to God. . . . "Now, Lord, consider their threats and enable your servants to speak your word with great boldness. Stretch out your hand to heal and perform signs and wonders through the name of your holy servant Jesus."
> ACTS 4:24, 29–30

God responded to their unity and their request. His answer was literally earthshaking:

> After they prayed, the place where they were meeting was shaken. And they were all filled with the Holy Spirit and spoke the word of God boldly.
> ACTS 4:31

Your Twenty-Eight Days to Powerful Prayer

There are several ways to apply the principle of united prayer. Here are a few:

- Pray with others about the same things *in different places at different times.*
- Pray with others for the same things *at the same time in different places.*
- Pray with others about the same things *in the same place at the same time.*

I suggest that you have a prayer partner or partners to pray with regularly. As I mentioned earlier, my wife and I try to pray together every night at ten. Two of my friends, Connie and Marilyn, both widows, call each other at the same time each day and pray together over the phone.

I also suggest that when you are facing big issues, call several people to join together to pray about those issues. Share the concerns and invite them to pray about them until you come to a place of agreement about God's answers. The group may meet together several times until the answer comes.

Beyond that, take advantage of the power of corporate prayer. Instead of merely making a long list of prayer requests, adjust your small group or Sunday school class to have a time when everyone actively agrees in prayer about one big thing.

Questions to Consider

1. When have you seen God moving as you prayed with others?
2. What does your prayer time with others look like?
3. What specifically can you begin doing to better apply the power of united prayer?

Notes

1. Charles Spurgeon, quoted by Wesley L. Duewel, *Mighty Prevailing Prayer* (Grand Rapids, Michigan: Zondervan). Kindle Edition, 139.
2. Adapted from Dave Earley, *28 Days to Knowing God* (Uhrichsville, Ohio: Barbour Publishing, 2019).

PRAYER BOOSTERS

Resolution in Prayer

One morning several years ago, I woke up with a horrible case of the flu. This illness hung on, and I lost eighteen pounds in three weeks. I began to feel a severe, steady pain in my joints and muscles, and I had a terrible headache that would not go away. I was suddenly allergic to all sorts of things. Also, my cognitive capacities would sometimes short circuit and I had great difficulty getting words to come out of my mouth. (This is not a good thing if you are a pastor.) I could not sleep for more than a few hours at a time. About five o'clock every evening, I would get a terrible sore throat and begin to feel waves of despair crowding into my soul.

Yet, none of that could compare with the extreme fatigue that I felt. I woke up exhausted and stayed that way all day long. I would lay in bed and concentrate on mustering all of my strength just so I could turn over by myself. I had been a varsity athlete in college, and yet at one point I was so weak that the only thing I could do for the day was crawl down the hall to the bathroom.

On top of all that, my church was going through a difficult period of transition. As the senior pastor, it was important for me to invest additional energy in helping navigate the church through the challenging waters it faced. Yet, I did not have any extra energy.

But worse than that was the awful guilt I felt because I couldn't function at home as a husband and father. At the time, my three boys were all under the age of five. They just could not understand why Dad could not play with them like he usually did or why he could not do things like go out and make a snowman. Also, my wife really needed me to help around the house. Yet, it was all I could do to take care of myself and try to keep working. I hated seeing my own exhaustion wearing her out too.

As the weeks went by, I grew frustrated at being the slave to my pain and fatigue. I am a goal-oriented person who was unable to pursue any goal other than survival. I lived like that for months before I told anyone or sought help. Eventually, I was diagnosed with an immunological disease doctors did not know much about at the time.

I became frustrated with God at this time in my life. Day after day, I asked for deliverance, or an explanation—or, at the very least, a time frame for my agony. But the only response I received was silence. . .blank, empty, hollow, deafening silence. Day after day, week after week, month after month, God said nothing.

I looked in the book of Job for a time frame. My question was, "How long did Job suffer?" I even asked some of the best Bible scholars in the country that question, and they all had the same answer: "The Bible does not say."

I felt as though God had abandoned me, and I did not even know why. My soul was dry and my heart was broken. I hate to admit it, but I eventually reasoned that if God would no longer speak to me, then I would not speak to Him. For a period of weeks, I had almost no prayer life.

But I knew this was wrong. I am a Christian and Christians "cannot not" pray. I am a child of God and children of God talk to their heavenly Father.

So little by little, I began to practice saying thanksgiving prayers and then prayers of praise. Then I did some intercessory prayers and liberation prayers.

I began to feel a little better.

"Even If. . ."

I finally started to turn the corner, helped by, of all things, a simple, direct message in a greeting card.

One day I got a card from my mom. My mom had plenty of health problems of her own, yet that did not stop her from serving God with her whole heart. The essence of the message she wrote in her card was, "Quit griping and get going again." As I read it, I almost laughed out loud.

Mom's card reminded me that I had come too far with God to give up on Him now. So finally, I began to pray what I call a prayer of resolution—or an "Even if. . ." prayer:

God, I will worship You and serve You *even if. . .*

Even if I never get well.

Even if You don't answer my prayers.

Even if You never give me an explanation.

As I prayed that way, an amazing thing happened. Over the next few weeks, I got noticeably better. It was a process that took time, but it was very real. Occasionally, I still have issues with my immune system (I got shingles three times in one year), but overall, I am very healthy now. I exercise almost an hour every day.

But *even if* I had not gotten better, *even if* I had only gotten worse, God would still be worthy of my loyalty and service. *Even if* He never said another thing to me, did another thing for me, gave another thing to me, He would still deserve all my love and devotion. The way I see it, I deserve eternal death, but He has given me eternal life and abundant life, so I owe Him everything I have.

One day I will be "all better"—and when I say "better" I mean *better!* I will walk the streets of heaven in a brand-new, pain-free, tireless, nonallergic, glorious, incorruptible body. No more fatigue! No more weakness! No more exhaustion! No more pain! I not only will be "as good as I used to be," but I will be *much better than I ever imagined!*

Until then, though, I will love, obey, and remain devoted to the God who has promised me that perfect, eternal body.

"Though He Slay Me"

As he always did, Job got up one morning and prayed. Yet, in a horrific next few hours, he received one report after another detailing the complete loss of his business and the death of all ten of his children. To make matters worse, the next day, his body was covered in screaming open wounds.

When Job looked for encouragement from his friends, all he got was accusation and condemnation. When he prayed, all he got from God was distance and silence. Job was painfully honest in voicing his frustration, disappointment, and questions. But he made a great decision that showed his true colors. In his anguish, Job offered a powerful prayer of resolution: "Though he slay me, yet will I hope in him" (Job 13:15).

"I Will. . ."

David and the other psalmists understood the power of resolution. Nearly two hundred times in the psalms, they declare, "I will." Many of these declarations of determination are prayers of resolution.

For example, as David ran for his life from the unjust insanity of King Saul and ended up hiding in a cave, he offered these powerful prayers of resolution, each containing the words "I will":

> I will bless the LORD at all times; his praise
> shall continually be in my mouth.
> PSALM 34:1 KJV

> In the shadow of Your wings I will make my refuge,
> until these calamities have passed by. I will cry out to
> God Most High, to God who performs all things for me. . . .
> My heart is steadfast, O God, my heart is steadfast; I will
> sing and give praise. . . . Awake, my glory! Awake, lute and
> harp! I will awaken the dawn. I will praise You, O Lord,
> among the peoples; I will sing to You among the nations.
> PSALM 57:1–2, 7–9 NKJV

> I will bless You while I live; I will lift up my hands
> in Your name. . . . Because You have been my help,
> therefore, in the shadow of Your wings I will rejoice.
> PSALM 63:4, 7 NKJV

Later, when David had to flee for his life into the wilderness a second time because his son Absalom tried to overthrow him, he again turned to the prayers of resolution:

My voice You shall hear in the morning, O LORD;
in the morning I will direct it to You, and I will look up.
PSALM 5:3 NKJV

But as for me, I will come into Your house in the
multitude of Your mercy; in fear of You I will
worship toward Your holy temple.
PSALM 5:7 NKJV

Praying the Prayer of Resolution

The prayer of resolution expresses loyalty to God in the face of His discipline, silence, or incomprehensible ways. It is a determination to continue to do the right thing no matter what is going on around you. It is a choice to refuse to hold a grudge toward God. It is stating that you trust the Lord enough to let Him take you beyond what you thought you could bear. It is returning unconditional, grateful loyalty for God's gift of unconditional love, even in terrible circumstances.

Your Twenty-Eight Days to Powerful Prayer

Is there an area where you need to offer a resolution in prayer? Some examples could be:

"Lord, I will worship and serve You *even if* . . .

- . . .my prayers are not answered."
- . . .my mate does not change."
- . . .my dreams do not come true."
- . . .I do not get the promotion."
- . . .my mother is not healed."
- . . .my child does not get born again."
- . . .I never meet 'Mr. or Miss Right.'"
- . . .I never receive an explanation for the adversity I am facing."

I suggest that you make the prayer of resolution a key part of your strategy to experience spiritual victory even when you face situational anarchy. But it will be easier to make the right choice *then* if you get into the habit of doing it *now*. Therefore, I also suggest that you make a few simple prayers of resolution an element of your daily prayers.

Questions to Consider

1. What resonated with you in this chapter? Why?
2. Are you currently facing some difficult situations or dealing with unanswered prayers?
3. How can resolution prayer help you?
4. What resolutions should you make now?

PRAYER BOOSTERS

When Prayer Goes Unanswered

Have you ever prayed, seriously prayed, about a matter, but received no answer?

Have you removed the roadblocks to answered prayer but still don't see a response to your request?

Are you living as right with God as you possibly can, but He still seems deaf to your pleas relating to something you're ardently praying about?

I understand. Because I've gone through those same things myself, I totally get it.

Waiting for an Answer. . .and Waiting Some More

I have been humbly, earnestly, desperately praying about a very important matter for several years but have received no answer. During this season of supernatural silence, I have carefully gone through the checklist of roadblocks to answered prayer (Day 15) and have done everything I can to meet the conditions for answered prayer. Yet no answers.

I have examined my motives. With boldness and faith, I have prayed confidently that God's answer to my request will accomplish *His* will, advance *His* kingdom, and glorify *His* name. But no answer has come.

I have diligently prayed scripture promises and have prayed scripture prayers over this matter. I have been careful to pray with thanksgiving and praise. I have forgiven everyone I can think of. I have repeatedly surrendered the issue to God. I even fasted for forty days, primarily to see a breakthrough in this one area. Yet there is no visible progress.

My wife and I have been united in prayer about this matter for over a year (Matthew 18:19–20). We have asked spiritually mature people to join us in praying for this request. Recognizing the reality of spiritual warfare, we have been persevering in prayer until a breakthrough comes.

All of that and, at least from my perspective, not much positive has happened. In fact, as I write this, some things have gotten worse.

Why? The answer may involve three important questions about unanswered prayer.

Three Important Questions

In my own life of prayer, I have learned that there are three important questions I should ask myself when my prayers are not being answered:

1. Is it me? When I believe I am asking for something legitimate and yet see no results, I ask God to show me *why* He is not answering. Sometimes the answer points right back to me. To put it another way, *I am the reason God has not answered my prayers*.

Maybe I am hanging onto a specific sin, or perhaps there is someone I have yet to forgive from my heart. Maybe I have prayed with selfish motives. Or, possibly, I have prayed in doubt and not faith.

The good news is that when I correct the problem, the answers come.

On some occasions, I have sensed that I needed to add fasting to the equation. After I fast and pray, I receive the answer.

2. Is it Satan? In Daniel 10 (see Day 22) we see that God sometimes sends the answer the moment we begin to pray. Sometimes, though, His answer is held up because the enemy is interfering. Satan often views the answer to prayer as especially damaging to his kingdom of darkness, so he fights to keep the answer from coming.

Remember, when spiritual warfare is holding up God's answer to prayer, that often means that the breakthrough is near. That's why it's important to persevere in praying until we receive the answer.

3. Is it God? There are times when nothing we do seems to make any difference. We pray and pray, yet the heavens are silent, God is distant, and our earnest request seems to have been totally ignored. Sometimes God Himself is the reason our prayers are not answered.

Let's take a look at that in more detail.

Six Reasons God Does Not Answer

There are several possible reasons for unanswered prayer that all revolve around God. Here are six things to consider about God when it seems He isn't answering your prayers:

1. God is Sovereign, so He does not need to explain Himself to us.

> The LORD does whatever pleases him, in the heavens
> and on the earth, in the seas and all their depths.
> PSALM 135:6

> Our God is in heaven; he does whatever pleases him.
> PSALM 115:3

God knew Job was a good and godly man, yet in a series of seemingly senseless attacks from the enemy, God allowed Job to lose everything.

Remarkably, Job responded with worship and prayer (Job 1:20–22). He also begged God for relief from his pain and for an explanation for this senseless ruin.

But God was silent.

Job's friends were no help. In fact, they falsely blamed Job for his suffering.

Yet Job maintained his faith and continued his prayers as he pleaded with God to give him an audience.

Finally, God appeared to Job (Job 40–41). But instead of letting Job air his griefs, instead of explaining His inactivity and silence, God gave Job a mini-tour of creation. Instead of Job getting to question God, God further crushed Job's pride by asking him a series of rhetorical questions. God's point was clear:

I am God. You are not. I do not need to explain Myself to you.

Job answered that he was convinced that God is sovereign and that he had no right to question Him (Job 42:1–6). Then he prayed for his self-righteous, judgmental friends.

That seemed to be just what God was looking for from Job. The next thing we see is the Lord taking up Job's defense before his friends, turning his situation around, and blessing him with twice as much as he had before (Job 42:7–16).

God is the sovereign Creator. He does not need to explain His activities, or lack of activities, to me, to you, or to anyone.

2. God's ways are not my ways, so I won't always understand why He does or does not do certain things.

> *"For my thoughts are not your thoughts, neither are your ways my ways," declares the* LORD. *"As the heavens are higher than the earth, so are my ways higher than your ways and my thoughts than your thoughts."*
> ISAIAH 55:8–9

God is infinite. We are not. He has unlimited knowledge. We do not. He has perfect understanding of all things. We don't. Therefore, God does things that are beyond our ability to grasp. When we are in heaven, we'll receive more understanding of God and His ways. But until that day, we will sometimes struggle to see or understand what God is doing:

> *For now we see only a reflection as in a mirror; then we shall see face to face. Now I know in part; then I shall know fully, even as I am fully known.*
> 1 CORINTHIANS 13:12

My dog cannot comprehend *why* I do some of the things I do. He does not understand why I don't always do the things *he* wants me to do. In his mind, I primarily exist to feed him, play with him, take him for rides in the car, and walk him. He cannot understand why I don't do those things more often.

But I am the man and he is the dog. I don't have to explain my activities to him. Even if I could, there are some things he just couldn't understand.

Likewise, I won't always understand why God does or does not do certain things, but I am alright with that. I could not fully worship a God I can fully understand.

3. God is eternal and perfectly patient, so He does not work according to my timetable. God is eternal (Deuteronomy 33:27; Psalm 102:12; Revelation 1:8). He dwells outside the realm of space and time. He lives in a never-ending present (Exodus 3:14). God is also patient. The Old Testament refers to God as a "compassionate and gracious God, slow to anger, abounding in love and faithfulness" (Exodus 34:6; also see Numbers 14:18; Nehemiah 9:6; Psalm 86:15, 103:8, 145:8; Joel 2:13).

Solomon stated that God has "a time for everything, and a season for every activity under the heavens" (Ecclesiastes 3:1). In speaking of God's patience, Peter reminded his readers that an eternal God views time differently than we do: "With the Lord a day is like a thousand years, and a thousand years are like a day" (2 Peter 3:8).

God does not work on our timetables. It may seem as though God's answer to you is taking an eternity to get to you, but He knows that is not the case—compared with eternity, it has been a mere blinking of an eye. God will answer when *He* sees fit.

Maybe we are asking for the right thing, but God knows that giving it to us now would be the wrong time. We need to be patient and trust His timing.

4. God does not always give us the little thing we want now because it might hinder the much bigger, better thing He wants to give us

later. Consider Joseph. He probably prayed something like, "Set me free from slavery," or later, "Get me out of prison." But God did not answer the way he wanted Him to. Yet, *because* God allowed Joseph to remain in prison, he was given an opportunity to interpret Pharaoh's dream. As a result, he became prime minister of Egypt. I am sure that it did not make sense to Joseph then, but it would later.

Consider Jesus. When He thought about the anguish He was about to endure on the Cross, He asked God to take this assignment away and deliver Him from the pain:

> *He went a little farther and fell on His face, and prayed, saying, "O My Father, if it is possible, let this cup pass from Me; nevertheless, not as I will, but as You will."*
> MATTHEW 26:39 NKJV

But the Father did not answer. He was silent. Why? Because He had a bigger perspective. Jesus saw the agony that lay immediately ahead, but the Father saw the greater glory of the salvation of the world and the greater elevation and exaltation of His Son.

5. God is wise, so He has a better plan.

> *"For I know the plans I have for you," declares the* LORD, *"plans to prosper you and not to harm you, plans to give you hope and a future. Then you will call on me and come and pray to me, and I will listen to you. You will seek me and find me when you seek me with all your heart."*
> JEREMIAH 29:11–13

We usually believe that what we ask God for is the very best for us. But God is smarter and wiser than we are. He is omniscient and has unlimited understanding (Psalm 147:5). He alone has infinite knowledge of all things past, present, and future—whether actual or potential. He knows all that can be known of everything that has, is, will, or could exist. Sometimes He knows things that we cannot see or understand (Romans 11:33):

> *The LORD will keep you from all harm—*
> *he will watch over your life.*
> PSALM 121:7

Sometimes the Lord does not answer the way we want Him to because He is protecting us from danger we can't see coming. Other times, He waits for the perfect timing to give us the best possible answer.

6. *God is more concerned about my godliness than my happiness.* Most of us know Romans 8:28, but few know Romans 8:29. Let's read them both:

> *And we know that in all things God works for the good*
> *of those who love him, who have been called according*
> *to his purpose. For those God foreknew he also predestined*
> *to be conformed to the image of his Son, that he might*
> *be the firstborn among many brothers and sisters.*
> ROMANS 8:28–29

When we read that God works in all things for "good" (Romans 8:28), we assume that "good" refers to things that make us happy. But to God, our "good" means making us more like Jesus: "conformed to the image of his Son." God may be slow in answering our requests because He is using the postponement of gratification to grow us up in Christ.

Your Twenty-Eight Days to Powerful Prayer

When you face unanswered prayer, it is important that you do not get discouraged and give up. Keep praying, keep seeking, keep asking, and God will answer *when* He wants, *how* He wants, and *as* He wants.

Trust Him!

Questions to Consider

1. Are any of your prayers going unanswered right now?
2. Who do you think may be the reason? You? Satan? God?
3. If you are the reason, what should you do?
4. If Satan is the reason, how should you respond?
5. If God is the reason, what do you think He might be up to?

PRAYER ISSUES

Prayer That Sparks War in the Heavens

What do you think happens in the heavens when we pray on earth?

Do angels play a role in prayer?

The answers to these questions are found in Daniel 10.

Daniel's Twenty-One Days of Prayer and Fasting

Daniel was an outstanding Jewish teenager the Babylonians abducted and took to serve in the king's administration. His wisdom, outstanding character, and God-given ability to interpret dreams caused him to rise to the status of prime minister.

Daniel was also a devoted follower and prophet of the Most High God. Because of his dual role, Daniel was highly interested in both the political future of the Jews and the nation of Babylon. He felt very burdened to begin to fast and pray for answers:

> At that time, I, Daniel, mourned for three weeks. I ate
> no choice food; no meat or wine touched my lips; and I
> used no lotions at all until the three weeks were over.
> DANIEL 10:2 3

Daniel fasted and prayed for three weeks. His fast was accomplished through the season of Passover and the Feast of Unleavened Bread. His was not the typical fast of abstaining from all food but not water. It was a twenty-one-day, modified fast (possibly because of his age, as he was in his mideighties at the time).

During this fast, he probably ate only fruits and vegetables, just as he did in the fast described in Daniel 1. Many people call this form of modified fasting the "Daniel Fast."

Though Daniel fasted and prayed, nothing happened for three weeks. But after those twenty-one days of silence from God, something finally happened, something *really* big: a fearsome heavenly warrior appeared (Daniel 10:4–9).

This astounding person was no ordinary man. He was an angel—probably Gabriel (see Daniel 8:16; 9:21). His appearance scared Daniel's servants so badly that they fled. Even though Daniel had seen angels before, the appearance of this one paralyzed him.

Then the angel spoke:

> *A hand touched me and set me trembling on my hands*
> *and knees. He said, "Daniel, you who are highly esteemed,*
> *consider carefully the words I am about to speak to you,*
> *and stand up, for I have now been sent to you." And*
> *when he said this to me, I stood up trembling.*
> DANIEL 10:10–11

What a relief! When the angel spoke to Daniel, he gave him a wonderful compliment: "you who are highly esteemed." God loves all of us, but this is something beyond that. The angel declared that God "highly esteemed" Daniel.

What does it take to be someone God highly esteems or treasures? I think the answer is simple—be someone who esteems and treasures God very highly. Daniel certainly fit that description.

Then the angel told Daniel that God had heard his prayers and that he had come to Daniel in response:

> *Then he continued, "Do not be afraid, Daniel. Since the first*
> *day that you set your mind to gain understanding and to*
> *humble yourself before your God, your words were heard,*
> *and I have come in response to them."*
> DANIEL 10:12

Do not be afraid. In the Bible, almost every time a human encounters an angel, the angel says, "Do not be afraid." Why? The Bible contains more than three hundred direct references to angels, and never are they described as beautiful young women or cute little babies with bows and arrows. Angels are huge, powerful, strong, supernatural, fear-inducing warriors.

Since the first day. From the very first day Daniel began to fast and pray, God heard what he had said and sent the angel in response. That is so encouraging because it shows us that God loves us and hears our prayers *from the moment* we begin to pray.

Your words were heard, and I have come in response to them. It is also encouraging that the angel said he came "in response to" Daniel's prayers. His prayers caused an answer to be sent and an angel to fly.

But if God heard and answered right away, why did it take three weeks before Daniel got an answer? Keep reading!

The Prince of the Persian Kingdom

The Bible tells us something very interesting about the reason for the delay in God's answer to Daniel—despite the prophet's persistent prayers:

> "But the prince of the Persian kingdom resisted me twenty-one days. Then Michael, one of the chief princes, came to help me, because I was detained there with the king of Persia. Now I have come to explain to you what will happen to your people in the future, for the vision concerns a time yet to come."
> DANIEL 10:13–14

But the prince of the Persian kingdom resisted me twenty-one days. This delay to Daniel's answer was unusual for him (In Daniel 9:20–21, the angel Gabriel came even as Daniel was praying the first day.) Why was Daniel's answer delayed this time?

The angel explained to Daniel that opposition had come from the prince of Persia. This prince had the power to prevent the angel from getting through to deliver the answer to Daniel's prayer.

Who is the prince of Persia? How could he stop an angel as formidable as the one who visited Daniel?

Clearly this was no human prince. No man who has ever lived is capable of stopping an angel of God. Rather, the angel was referring to a specific rank of fallen angel or high-ranking demon called a "principality." Angels and demons are military beings who engage in spiritual warfare over the souls of men. Paul mentions some of the ranks of demons in his letter to the Ephesians:

> Put on the whole armor of God, that you may be able to
> stand against the wiles of the devil. For we do not wrestle
> against flesh and blood, but against principalities, against
> powers, against the rulers of the darkness of this age,
> against spiritual hosts of wickedness in the heavenly places.
> Ephesians 6:11–12 NKJV

The prince of Persia wasn't a mere human prince but the high-ranking demon principality that had authority over the nation of Persia, where Daniel lived. I believe the resistance from the demon prince of Persia was not the work of one demon, but of that demon and his entire demonic army.

Then Michael, one of the chief princes, came to help me, because I was detained there with the king of Persia. When the prince of Persia and his forces delayed the angel, God sent another angel, Michael the archangel. Michael probably had his own army of angel warriors. They were able to break through the Persian defenses. Gabriel was then able to deliver the answer to Daniel. The answer was a great prophetic vision (see Daniel 11–12).

Prayer Lessons from Daniel

As we read this story, we learn five important, instructive, encouraging truths about prayer:

1. When we pray, God often sends answers right away. When answers are slow to arrive, I sometimes wonder if God has heard me. . .or if He is not responding to my desperate pleas for some specific reason. I am encouraged to pray when I remember that *from the very moment* Daniel began to fast and pray, God heard and later sent an answer.

2. Prayer can spark spiritual warfare. When you pray, you may be doing more than getting a load off your chest. You could be causing angels and demons to fly, spiritual armies to fight, and war to break out in the heavens. When I get to heaven, I hope to see the video of the spiritual battle that was kicked up over Persia because of Daniel's prayer.

3. Spiritual warfare may hinder answered prayer. Why, sometimes, does seemingly nothing happen when we pray? According to Daniel 10, it could be because of spiritual warfare. Maybe God has already sent an angel with your answer, but the enemy responded by sending demon interference to oppose the angel and keep the answer from breaking through. That is yet another reason to persevere in prayer.

4. Persistence in prayer and fasting aids answered prayer. Daniel persevered in praying and fasting for twenty-one days *before* his answer arrived. He never gave up but instead prayed until something happened.

I wonder what would have happened had Daniel stopped praying before the answer came. Would God have sent Michael to help? Would the angel with the answer have been able to get through?

5. Fasting may be a significant aid in answered prayer. We will discuss fasting more in Day 26, but for now we need to understand that an incredible set of events occurred when Daniel humbled himself through fasting (Daniel 10:12).

Your Twenty-Eight Days to Powerful Prayer

Amazing things happen when we pray. Answers to prayers may be sent and spiritual warfare may be going on. Angels get involved, with good angels aiding the delivery of answers to prayer and evil angels, or demons, hindering answers to prayer.

Have you ever felt God impressing you to pray for something, but the answer did not come even after many days of asking? If so, it may be that the answer is being held up because of spiritual warfare. Keep on praying. If need be, add fasting. In God's time, your answer will break through.

Questions to Consider

1. What did you learn from this story of Daniel?
2. How does studying this story make you feel? Why?
3. What in this story encouraged your prayer life?

PRAYER ISSUES

Praying for Spiritual Leaders

Being a spiritual leader can be hazardous to personal and family well-being.[1] The pressures of full-time ministry are often intense. Harsh critics, tight finances, long hours, family challenges, and spiritual attack can make the leader feel suffocated.

Spiritual leaders carry a greater load of responsibility than those who are not leaders. They also suffer greater spiritual attack. Beyond that, the enemy targets leaders for increased temptation. That's why they need all of us to pray for them. . .and why those of us who are spiritual leaders should not to be too proud to ask others to pray for us.

Even many of the Bible's greatest leaders needed the support of other believers. Let's look at one great example from way back in Old Testament times.

Moses, Aaron, and Hur

Moses already had a tough assignment. God had called him to lead the massive, messy, rowdy rabble of Israelites through the wilderness on their way to the Promised Land. Then, to make things even more complicated, the Amalekites attacked them.

This was not good news, considering the fact that the Israelites didn't even have an army.

Moses ordered Joshua to gather some men and go face the Amalekites in battle. Instead of going out himself to fight, Moses went to the top of a hill overlooking the battlefield. He stood on the hill between the battle and the Lord. As he did, he held up his hands as a symbol of prayer (see 1 Timothy 2:8). In one of his hands, he held what may have been the staff God used as an instrument of miracles in the Israelites' deliverance from the Egyptians (see Exodus 7:19–20; 8:5–6; 8:16–17).

Amazingly, the ragtag army of Israel was successful. . .but only as long as Moses held up his hands in prayer. When Moses' arms got tired, the army started to lose:

> So Joshua fought the Amalekites as Moses had ordered, and Moses, Aaron and Hur went to the top of the hill. As long as Moses held up his hands, the Israelites were winning, but whenever he lowered his hands, the Amalekites were winning.
> EXODUS 17:10–11

Fortunately, two men—Aaron and Hur, both important leaders themselves—took seriously their responsibility to support their spiritual leader. *Their* efforts supported Moses so that *his* prayers could support Joshua. That made the difference between defeat and victory:

> When Moses' hands grew tired, they took a stone and put it under him and he sat on it. Aaron and Hur held his hands up— one on one side, one on the other—so that his hands remained steady till sunset. So Joshua overcame the Amalekite army with the sword.
> EXODUS 17:12–13

What a vivid picture of the power of intercessory prayer by spiritual leaders *for* spiritual leaders. The army enjoyed victory only when Moses held up his hands in prayer for them. But Moses had the strength to pray for them only when two leaders held up his hands.

E. M. Bounds retired from his busy life as a successful lawyer, pastor, editor, and evangelist to give the last seventeen years of his life to prayer and writing about prayer. He rose daily at four a.m. and prayed until seven a.m. Regarding the scene recorded in Exodus 17, he wrote, "We have a striking picture of the preacher's need for prayer, and of what a people's prayers can do for him."[2] In another one of his books, Bounds said, "It is absolutely necessary for the preacher to pray. It is absolutely necessary for the preacher to be prayed for."[3]

Untapped Power

Does praying for spiritual leaders make a difference?

A study was conducted of 130 pastors, evangelists, and missionaries who had trained prayer warriors praying for them fifteen minutes a day for one year. Eighty-nine percent of those surveyed stated that the prayers had a positive effect on their ministry. They reported personal advancement as shown by better attitudes, improved personal prayer lives, more spiritual discernment and wisdom, increased leadership skills, and enhanced effectiveness in using their spiritual gifts. They also saw a greater response to their ministry, as 60 percent indicated that their churches grew in numbers through reaching the unchurched. (One pastor said his church grew from fifteen to six hundred people.) The study also showed that daily prayer for the spiritual leaders was more effective than weekly or monthly prayer.

The study concluded:

> There exists a tremendous reservoir of untapped prayer power in every church which can be affirmed, trained, and deployed to see the lost won, the apathetic revived, the "backslider" restored, and the committed made more effective.[4]

Former missionary and professor Peter Wagner agreed: "The most underutilized source of spiritual power in our churches today is intercession for Christian leaders."[5]

Pray for Me

The apostle Paul endured horrible trials for the cause of Christ. He faced severe hardship, opposition, pressure, and persecution.

He suffered hunger, thirst, shipwreck, critics, mob violence, beatings, whippings, and imprisonments (2 Corinthians 11:23–28). He also faced intense spiritual opposition (2 Corinthians 12:9).

Paul, however, was also a model of incredible spiritual effectiveness. He took the gospel to the cities around the Mediterranean Sea and planted dozens of new churches. Beyond that, he wrote thirteen letters that became books in our New Testament.

What empowered Paul to have such a huge impact, even as he endured such deprivation and adversity? Paul consistently solicited people to pray for him:

> *Brothers and sisters, pray for us.*
> 1 THESSALONIANS 5:25

> *As for other matters, brothers and sisters, pray for us*
> *that the message of the Lord may spread rapidly*
> *and be honored, just as it was with you.*
> 2 THESSALONIANS 3:1

> *I urge you, brothers and sisters, by our Lord Jesus*
> *Christ and by the love of the Spirit, to join me*
> *in my struggle by praying to God for me.*
> ROMANS 15:30

> *Pray also for me, that whenever I speak,*
> *words may be given me so that I will fearlessly*
> *make known the mystery of the gospel.*
> EPHESIANS 6:19

> *And pray for us, too, that God may open a door*
> *for our message, so that we may proclaim the*
> *mystery of Christ, for which I am in chains.*
> COLOSSIANS 4:3

Prayer Partners

Noted Christian author Max Lucado is a longtime pastor. After being convinced of the importance of having other believers pray for him as a spiritual leader, he recruited 120 "Prayer Part-ners" to "pray *for* him daily and pray *with* him fervently." Apart from praying for him each day, 30 of them arrived at the church early one Sunday per month to pray for the congregation.

After the first six months of the project, Lucado wrote,

> *Has God honored the prayers of his people? Here is a sam-ple of what God has done since we organized the Prayer Partners.*
> - *We have broken our Sunday attendance record twice.*
> - *We have finished the year with our highest ever Sunday attendance.*
> - *We have finished the year—hang onto your hat—over budget.*
> - *We have added three new staff members and six elders.*
> - *We witnessed several significant healings.*
> - *Our church antagonism is down, and church unity is high.*
> - *More significantly we called our church to forty days of prayer and fasting, inviting God to shine his face on his people.*
>
> *More than ever, I am convinced. When we work, we work; but when we pray God works.*[6]

Mighty Men

When I was leading my first church, I became convicted that I needed to get past my pride and invite people in my congrega-tion to pray for me. I developed a team of twelve men to serve as what we called Mighty Men of Prayer. I asked them to make a one-year commitment to:

- Pray for our church, themselves, and their family daily.
- Take a few minutes of extra time to pray for me one day a week.
- Take a few minutes every Saturday night to pray for me.

Every two weeks, I met with these men for Bible study and prayer. At these meetings, I would share with them my prayer requests for the next two weeks. Their prayers made a positive difference in my life and ministry.

Because what we were doing was so successful, the next year I expanded our prayer team to twenty-five men. That year was even better than the first, so I doubled the number to fifty on my prayer team over the next few years. Several of the prayer partners decided to meet on Sunday mornings in the prayer room and also pray during the worship services. The results were astounding. Our church baptized more people, grew more, developed more leaders, and planted more churches than ever before.

Your Twenty-Eight Days to Powerful Prayer

I encourage you to make a commitment to pray for your pastor or spiritual mentor daily, even if your prayer is only a few sentences. Some of the areas you can pray for include:

- Wisdom
- Purity
- Spiritual passion
- Vision and leadership decisions
- Marriage
- Children
- Health
- Finances

If you are a spiritual leader, I encourage you to pray about whom you should ask to be a member of your prayer team. Start by recruiting one or two prayer partners. Regularly communicate with them the needs you want them to pray about. Also, be sure to reciprocate by praying for them regularly.

Questions to Consider

1. What surprised you most about this chapter?

2. Have you made it your practice to pray for your spiritual leader(s)?

3. If you are a spiritual leader, have you developed an active and effective prayer team?

Notes

1. H. B London, Jr. and Neil Wiseman, *Pastors at Greater Risk* (Ventura, California: Regal Books, 2003), 33–60.

2. E. M. Bounds, *The Weapon of Prayer* (Grand Rapids, Michigan: Revell, 1931), 125.

3. E. M. Bounds, *Power Through Prayer* (Grand Rapids, Michigan: Baker Book House, 1972), 75–76.

4. Nancy Pfaff, "Christian Leadership Attributes Dynamic Increase in Effectiveness to the Work of Intercession," *Journal of the American Society for Church Growth*, 1990 edition, 82.

5. Peter Wagner, *Prayer Shield* (Ventura, California: Regal Books, 1992), 9.

6. Max Lucado, quoted in John Maxwell, *Partners in Prayer* (Nashville, Tennessee: Thomas Nelson, 1996), foreword.

DAY 24

PRAYER ISSUES

Praying with Paul for Others

When I was a child, my parents took me to Sunday school. One week in class, the teacher encouraged us to pray for our family members daily. I decided that was a good idea, so that night as I lay in bed, I prayed for them: "God, please bless Mom. God bless Dad. God bless Carol, and God bless Steve—he really needs it."

My prayer was short, sweet, simple, and sufficient for a child. But when I got older and read the Bible, I realized that the apostle Paul's prayers were on an entirely different level from mine.

Fortunately for us today, Paul recorded a sampling of his prayers in the letters he wrote (see Romans 1:8–10; 15:5–6, 13; 1 Corinthians 1:4–7; Ephesians 1:15–19, 3:14–19; Philippians 1:3–11; Colossians 1:3–12; 1 Thessalonians 1:2–3; 3:11–13; 2 Thessalonians 1:11–12; Philemon 4–6). Taken together, these prayers are a master's class on how to pray for others.

The Big Picture

One evening, I read all of Paul's prayers for others found in his letters. Reading them in one sitting helped me see four characteristics of prayer each of us should practice:

1. Pray thankfully. In nearly all of his prayers, Paul mentioned his gratitude to God for the ones he was praying for. He repeatedly mentioned how thankful he was for his spiritual children and how grateful he was for the work God had already done and was doing in them.

- To the church at Rome, he wrote, "First, I thank my God through Jesus Christ for all of you, because your faith is being reported all over the world" (Romans 1:8).
- To the Corinthians he said, "I always thank my God for you because of his grace given you in Christ Jesus" (1 Corinthians 1:4).
- To the Ephesian church, "Ever since I heard about your faith in the Lord Jesus and your love for all God's people, I have not stopped giving thanks for you, remembering you in my prayers" (Ephesians 1:15–16).
- To the Philippians he stated, "I thank my God every time I remember you. In all my prayers for all of you, I always pray with joy" (Philippians 1:3–4).
- To the Colossians, "We always thank God, the Father of our Lord Jesus Christ, when we pray for you" (Colossians 1:3).
- To the church in Thessalonica, "We always thank God for all of you and continually mention you in our prayers" (1 Thessalonians 1:2–3; see also 1 Thessalonians 2:13; 1 Thessalonians 3:9; 2 Thessalonians 1:3).
- To the young pastor Timothy, he wrote, "I thank God, whom I serve, as my ancestors did, with a clear conscience, as night and day I constantly remember you in my prayers" (2 Timothy 1:3).
- To the former slave-owner Philemon, Paul said, "I always thank my God as I remember you in my prayers" (Philemon 4).

As I read through each prayer and noted for whom it was given, one group leaps off the page at me the Corinthians. These Christians gave Paul fits by making immature decisions, fighting with each other, disrespecting his role in their lives, and rebelling against his leadership. Yet in his two lengthy letters to them, he showed no bitterness. Instead, he always thanked God for them and for the work He had done in their lives.

I was not only amazed by the fact that he was consistently

grateful for the ones he prayed for, but also surprised at the reasons for his gratitude. Not once did he say that he was grateful for their health, wealth, or prosperity, and he made no mention of their physical or material blessings. Rather, Paul focused on their *spiritual* blessings. He repeatedly stated that he was thankful to God for what He had done in their lives, what He was doing in their lives, and what He would do in their lives in the future.

Of course, it is appropriate to thank God for the physical, material, educational, vocational, and relational blessings He gives the ones we love. But the primary focus of our gratitude should be on the spiritual work He has done, is doing, and is yet to do in their lives.

2. Pray consistently. Paul was very consistent in his prayers. When you read the prayers in his letters, you can see the repetition of many phrases describing the frequency of his prayers for his spiritual children: "without ceasing," "always," "do not cease," "always," "without ceasing," "night and day," "exceedingly," "always," "without ceasing," "day and night." Every time these believers came to Paul's mind, he thanked God for them and offered a prayer on their behalf.

Most Christians tend to do the bulk of their praying in response to a crisis. But when there is no urgency, we tend to pray with less frequency and fervency. (Maybe if we prayed more when there was no emergency, we might have fewer emergencies.)

We think about, talk to, and spend time with our loved ones. But we should also set aside time to pray for them consistently—whether or not they are going through difficult times. It's a good idea to set aside a given time, at least once a day, to pray for your loved ones. My wife and I do—we have a standing date at ten every night to pray for our children.

3. Pray expectantly. I love Paul's confidence as he prayed for believers in the churches he had started or visited. He believed that God was not finished with these people, that He had more and better things on the way. He made it clear that the basis of His confidence was in the fact that *God is faithful*.

Note these examples:

May the God of hope fill you with all joy and peace as you trust in him, so that you may overflow with hope by the power of the Holy Spirit. I myself am convinced, my brothers and sisters, that you yourselves are full of goodness, filled with knowledge and competent to instruct one another.
ROMANS 15:13–14

In all my prayers for all of you, I always pray with joy because of your partnership in the gospel from the first day until now, being confident of this, that he who began a good work in you will carry it on to completion until the day of Christ Jesus.
PHILIPPIANS 1:4–6

Now to him who is able to do immeasurably more than all we ask or imagine, according to his power that is at work within us, to him be glory in the church and in Christ Jesus throughout all generations, for ever and ever! Amen.
EPHESIANS 3:20–21

As I read these prayers, I realize that too often the aim of my own prayers is much too low. Paul prayed with the expectation that God would do wonderful things in people's lives. He believed that God was able and willing to work and could do more than expected.

We too can pray for others with great expectation because we pray to a great and faithful God.

4. Pray spiritually. Paul focused his prayers on people's spiritual progress. Here are several of the many spiritual requests Paul made of God on behalf of others:

- Live in harmony with others (Romans 15:5–6)

- Be filled with joy, peace, and spiritual energy (Romans 15:13)
- Know God personally (Ephesians 1:17)
- Know what God is calling them to do and be (Ephesians 1:18)
- Be inwardly strengthened with Spirit-imparted power (Ephesians 3:16)
- Open their hearts fully to Christ (Ephesians 3:17)
- Have an increasing realization of Christ's extravagant love for them (Ephesians 3:18)
- Be full of God (Ephesians 3:19)
- Have abundant and discerning love (Philippians 1:9)
- Prioritize the things that matter (Philippians 1:10)
- Be blameless and pure (Philippians 1:10)
- Display the fruit of righteousness (Philippians 1:11)
- Clearly know and do God's will (Colossians 1:9)
- Choose to live worthy of the Lord (Colossians 1:10)
- Strive to please God in everything (Colossians 1:10)
- Be fruitful in good works (Colossians 1:10)
- Know God (Colossians 1:10)
- Have spiritual strength and endurance (Colossians 1:11)
- Explode in love (1 Thessalonians 3:12)
- Be filled with strength and holiness (1 Thessalonians 3:13)
- Be holy inside and out (1 Thessalonians 5:23)

I am sure Paul occasionally prayed for people's physical, material, and vocational needs. But what surprises me as I read his prayers was that the majority of his requests were for their spiritual condition. He also prayed that they would not remain at their current levels of spiritual maturity but instead grow, increase, and abound. I like the fact that the focus of his prayers was on the things that really matter, the things that last forever.

Your Twenty-Eight Days to Powerful Prayer

Pray consistently: Pray for several people every day. You can pray for the same people each day or a different group each day.

Pray thankfully: Start each prayer by being thankful for those you pray for.

Pray expectantly: For a few of your key people, pick a promise from God and expectantly pray it for them each day.

Pray spiritually: Pick one of Paul's prayers for each of your closest family members and pray it consistently for them during the next twenty-eight days.[1]

Questions to Consider

1. With how many of Paul's prayers were you already familiar?
2. What stood out to you as you considered his prayers?
3. Which of the four characteristics of Paul's prayers (Paul prayed thankfully, expectantly, consistently, and spiritually) do you think you most need to apply in your prayer life?

Notes

1. For more information about praying for loved ones, see *Praying for Your Children* by Elmer Towns and David Earley (Shippensburg, Pennsylvania: Destiny Image, 2011).

DAY 25

PRAYER ISSUES

Praying the Scriptures

Does your mind sometimes wander when you pray? Do you feel as though your prayers lack focus? Do you feel as though your prayers lack power?

If so, then try this: pray the scriptures!

To see how that works, read on!

Fifty Thousand Answered Prayers

Possibly the most powerful person of prayer in the modern era is George Mueller. In response to his prayers, God sent resources Mueller needed to care for 10,024 orphans during his lifetime and to establish 117 schools that offered Christian education to more than 120,000 children. He did this without advertising and without incurring debt.

Mueller also circulated 111 million Bible tracts and pamphlets, 1.4 million New Testaments, and 275,000 Bibles in different languages, along with nearly as many smaller portions of scripture. He financially supported 189 missionaries. After he turned seventy, he preached the gospel in forty-two nations to approximately three million people.

How was all that possible? Why was Mueller so effective? The short answer is prayer. In his journals, Mueller recorded more than *fifty thousand* answered prayers. But Mueller also took his communication with God to a different level, reading through the Bible nearly two hundred times, mixing prayer with his reading.

Mueller once said that during the first few years of his Christian life, he struggled to focus and pray for any length of time. But, he said, when he began to pray the scriptures, he rarely struggled to pray but instead deepened his communion with the Father and began to see more answers to his prayers.[1]

A Simple Way to Pray

When I was a young Christian, I read about Mueller's prayer life and was challenged to pray the scriptures. He once said that as he read the scriptures, "After a few minutes my soul was led to confession, or to thanksgiving, or to intercession, or to supplication."[2]

That sounded great to me, but I was not quite sure how to do it. . .until I read a book by Martin Luther.

Martin Luther was a husband, father, pastor, professor, author, and the highly influential leader of the Protestant Reformation. He began each of his long, busy days with several hours of prayer. After a friend asked him for practical advice about prayer, Luther wrote *A Simple Way to Pray, for a Good Friend*. It was first published nearly five hundred years ago, but its influence continues today.

In the book, Luther counseled using the Lord's Prayer, the psalms, and the Ten Commandments as models and guidelines in structuring prayer. He recommended praying through them phrase by phrase:

> With practice one can take the Ten Commandments on one day, a psalm or chapter of Holy Scripture the next day, and use them as flint and steel to kindle a flame in the heart.[3]

Luther taught that prayer could be like a garland of four twisted strands. Each strand could be posed as a question and an element of prayer. The four questions are:

1. What is the teaching in this passage for me?

2. What prayer of thanksgiving does this prompt?
3. What confession does it evoke?
4. What is the prayer petition that arises?

Praying the Psalms

After I became a Christian, I roller-coastered up and down for a year and a half. Then, as a freshman in college, I made a commitment to spend an hour a day with God, Monday through Friday. As I explained in Day 2, my plan was to spend a half hour reading, meditating, and praying through the psalms. Then I would spend another thirty minutes praying through my prayer lists and whatever else God laid on my heart.

Every day at noon, I sat down and pulled out my Bible, my notebook, and pen. Then I would read a psalm, meditate on it, pray through it, and then pray through my prayer lists. Specifically, my plan worked like this:

- Open the Bible and read the psalm of the day (for example, Psalm 23).
- Write down the date at the top of the page.
- Record one or two key verses from the psalm of the day. For example:

The Lord is my shepherd, I lack nothing. He makes me lie down in green pastures, he leads me beside quiet waters, he refreshes my soul.
Psalm 23:1–3

- Prayerfully ask the Lord what He had for me from those verses.
- Record a sentence or two of praise, thanksgiving, confession, supplication, and intercession the psalm prompted. Back to Psalm 23:1–3:

Thank You, Lord, for being my Shepherd. Thank you for meeting my needs, guiding my life, and refreshing my soul. I need it.

I praise You because You are truly the Good Shepherd.

I confess that I am impatient with Your timing in meeting my needs.

I ask you to help me get an A on my English test. I ask for money to pay my school bill next semester.

I ask You to be very active to draw my mom to Yourself today.

- Pray over what I had written, offering praise and thanks, confession, supplication, and intercession as appropriate.

By the time I had covered one page of the notebook, my heart would be encouraged and my soul filled. Then I would switch and begin to pray through the requests on my prayer lists.

When I first began praying the scriptures, it felt mechanical. But after a week or so, the biblical prompts of praise, thanksgiving, and so forth became launching points into spontaneous, open-hearted prayers. The hour I spent with the Lord each day flew, and the enjoyment increased.

See How Easy?

Maybe the system Martin Luther used seems overly rigid and clumsy to you. No worries: praying the Bible does not need to be complicated. Southern Seminary professor Donald Whitney states, "To pray the Bible, you simply go through the passage line by line, talking to God about whatever comes to mind as you read the text. See how easy it is? Anyone can do it."[4]

Whitney continues, "If you don't understand the meaning of that verse, go on to the next verse. If the meaning of that one is perfectly clear, but nothing comes to mind to pray about, go on to the next verse."[5]

Whitney testified that praying the scriptures is his secret to overcoming the struggle of not feeling like praying: "I can testify to the fact that having prayed this way almost every day for more than thirty years, there is nothing in my devotional life that more quickly and consistency kindles my consistently cold heart like praying the Bible."[6]

Regarding praying the scriptures, one saint of days gone by gave these words of advice:

> *Plunge into the very depths of the words you read until revelation, like a sweet aroma, breaks out upon you. . . .little by little you will come to experience a very rich prayer that flows from your inward being. . . . In praying the scripture, you are seeking to find the Lord in what you are reading, in the very words themselves.*[7]

Your Twenty-Eight Days to Powerful Prayer

If you want to learn to pray the scriptures, I suggest beginning with the psalms. They are the inspired hymnbook of the people of God. God gave them to us that we might give them back to Him in worship and prayer (Ephesians 5:18–19; Colossians 3:16). You start at Psalm 1 and pray through one psalm a day. If you start into a psalm and nothing comes to mind to pray about, you can go on to the next psalm.

Other than the psalms, I also have really enjoyed praying through Isaiah 40–66.

I have also prayed through the New Testament.

Questions to Consider

1. What did you especially like or learn from this chapter?
2. Have you ever prayed the scriptures?
3. Do you pray the scriptures on a regular basis?
4. How can you begin praying the scriptures daily?

Notes

1. Taken from *Spiritual Secrets of George Mueller* by Roger Steer (Wheaton, Illinois: Harold Shaw Publishers, 1992), 61–62.
2. Ibid, 61.

3. Martin Luther, *A Simple Way to Pray* (Louisville, Kentucky: Westminster Knox Press, 2000), 56.
4. Donald Whitney, *Praying the Bible* (Wheaton, Illinois: Crossway, 2015), 33.
5. Ibid.
6. Donald Whitney, *Praying the Bible*, 85.
7. Jeanne Guyon, *Experiencing God Through Prayer* (New Kensington, Pennsylvania: Whitaker House, 1984), 17.

DAY 26

PRAYER ISSUES

Prayer and Fasting

How much do you know about Christian fasting? Have you ever fasted for spiritual purposes? Do you fast as a spiritual discipline as a regular part of your Christian life?

If you've never fasted, then I'd encourage you to give it a try. After all, Jesus expected His followers to fast as a lifestyle.

"When You Fast. . ."

Have you ever been reading the Bible when something jumped out at you that you had never noticed before? I have! Several years ago, I was reading Jesus' sermon in Matthew 6 when something caught my attention. One word leaped out at me as if written in neon lights, and it's in each of these three verses:

> *"So when you give to the needy. . ."*
> MATTHEW 6:2

> *"And when you pray. . ."*
> MATTHEW 6:5

> *"When you fast. . ."*
> MATTHEW 6:16

"When you give. . .*when* you pray. . .*when* you fast." Jesus spoke the words in the above verses assuming that His followers would give to the poor and pray, and He also assumed that they would

fast. We all agree that giving to the poor and prayer should be regular parts of a healthy Christian life. But Jesus included fasting as equally essential and important as giving and praying.

When I began studying Christian fasting, I was surprised to discover that first-century Christians fasted two days a week—Wednesday and Friday. This means that if you were a follower of Jesus during the first few hundred years after His birth, you would fast from sundown Tuesday to dinner on Wednesday, since the early church operated on the Jewish paradigm of having a new day beginning at sunset. Then you might also fast from sundown Thursday to dinner Friday.

A Simple Spiritual Practice

The word *fasting* as it is used in the Bible (both Old and New Testament) means "not to eat" or "self-denial." A normal fast involved abstaining from all food, but not from water (Matthew 4:2).

A partial fast is the restriction of one's diet but not the complete abstention from all food. There are examples in the Old Testament of people severely limiting their diets while fasting. For example, Daniel limited himself to simple fruits and vegetables when he fasted (Daniel 1, 10).

Fasting can also involve abstaining from certain activities. Today, that might mean forgoing different forms of media or communication, such as television, movies, our phones, and the internet.

In the Bible, some fasts lasted from three days to forty days. Scripture also includes both individual and corporate fasts. An individual fast was something one person did as part of his or her Christian walk, while a corporate fast could involve the whole church (Acts 13:1–4) or even an entire nation (Jonah 3; Esther 4; 2 Chronicles 20).

The great thing about fasting is that anyone can fast in some way. If for some reason your health limits you from a full fast, you can fast from selected foods. If you can't do that, you can fast from specific activities.

Fasting is a doable spiritual practice. It is very simple: *Don't eat. Pray instead.*

Why Fast?

When I began studying fasting, I started out trying to answer the question *Why should I fast?* I studied every Bible passage having to do with fasting, and I discovered more than two dozen powerful examples of the benefits of fasting. Let's take a look at seven of them:

1. Fasting led to Hannah receiving a long-awaited answer to prayer (1 Samuel 1). Hannah had been unable to have a child for a long time, but after a special season of intense prayer and fasting, "the Lord remembered her." She got pregnant and conceived a special son, Samuel, whose name means "God heard." This boy, whose name was a reminder of answered prayer, became a great prophet and leader who shook the nation with his prayers.

Several years ago, I preached on Hannah's fasting and praying for a son. A lady named Rhonda, who was new to our church, had a daughter named Megan, whom she had not heard from in more than six months. Rhonda, a new Christian, began to fast and pray for Megan.

A few days later, Rhonda's phone rang. The voice on the other end said, "Hi, Mom. This is Megan." They got together, Megan started coming to church, and I baptized her a few months later.

That's the power of fasting in action!

2. Fasting and prayer aided in giving Jehoshaphat and his people an unbelievable victory (2 Chronicles 20). Three armies surrounded the nation of Judah and defeat looked certain, so King Jehoshaphat called his people to fasting and prayer. As a result, God gave them a crazy battle plan involving marching out to face the enemy while singing songs of praise and thanksgiving to the Lord. The moment they began to sing, God set ambushes against the enemy and defeated them all. Israel did not lose a man.

3. Fasting and prayer gave Nehemiah favor with the king of Persia (Nehemiah 1).

The mighty empire of Babylon had crushed the city of Jerusalem and took some of its people captive to serve in the capital city. Later, a Jewish man named Nehemiah was working for the king of Persia, which had defeated the Babylonian Empire. Nehemiah received news that the city of Jerusalem was further decimated and that the wall lay in ruin and reproach.

Nehemiah knew that the city would never be able to get back on its feet until the wall around it was rebuilt, so he fasted and prayed. As a result, God gave him the plan, the protection, and the provision he needed to do the impossible job.

4. Fasting yields mighty blessings (Isaiah 58:6-9).

Ancient Israel was often guilty of empty, external religion. Isaiah records the Lord's rebuke regarding their abuse of fasting. In doing so, he reveals several benefits of properly motived fasting:

> "Is not this the kind of fasting I have chosen: to loose the chains of injustice and untie the cords of the yoke, to set the oppressed free and break every yoke? Is it not to share your food with the hungry and to provide the poor wanderer with shelter—when you see the naked, to clothe them, and not to turn away from your own flesh and blood? Then your light will break forth like the dawn, and your healing will quickly appear; then your righteousness will go before you, and the glory of the Lord will be your rear guard. Then you will call, and the Lord will answer; you will cry for help, and he will say: Here am I."
> Isaiah 58:6-9

5. Fasting may be a secret service to God that leads to open rewards (Matthew 6:4, 6, 18).

Jesus promised that serving the poor and praying and fasting without fanfare brought open rewards from God. Those rewards could be answers to our prayers or the rich reward of more of God's presence. . .or crowns we can cast at Jesus' feet to say thanks.

6. *Fasting is a spiritual service (Luke 2:37).* Anna was a widow in her eighties who "worshiped night and day, fasting and praying" (Luke 2:37). This shows us that fasting can be a spiritual service most adults, even elderly ones, can perform.

Several years ago, I was speaking for a conference of missionaries. I was sitting at a table having lunch with some retired missionaries who had served in Iran.

"Do you miss your ministry in Iran?" I asked them.

One of them looked at me with a smile and said, "Young man, we have more ministry than ever because we have the time to fast and pray here and see God answer there."

7. *Fasting increases spiritual power and prepares for greater impact (Luke 4:1–14).* Prior to His forty-day fast, Jesus did no miracles and preached no sermons. But immediately after His fast, "Jesus returned to Galilee in the power of the Spirit" (Luke 4:14) and launched His powerful public ministry.

Why Am I Not Fasting?

After reading these and a dozen other reasons to fast, I changed my thinking from "Why should I fast?" to "Why am I *not* fasting more often?" At that time, I was extremely burdened over several situations so I launched a three-day season of prayer and fasting. Within the next thirty days, I received these stunning answers to prayer:

- Three young men who were critically injured in an automobile accident were healed.
- I received an unexpected check in the mail that provided me enough money to pay off the college bills for two of my friends so they could remain in school.
- I led exactly fifty teenagers to Christ in a thirty-day period.

Your Twenty-Eight Days to Powerful Prayer

Maybe you're facing a situation that has taken you to the point of desperation. Or maybe you want to deal with a situation before it gets that far. Why not set aside meals for a day, or even a few days, to seek the Lord about your situation with prayer and fasting?

Questions to Consider

1. What did this chapter teach you about fasting?
2. Have you ever fasted as a spiritual discipline?
3. How do you think fasting can benefit your prayer life?

PRAYER ISSUES

Praying in a Spiritual Desert

Is prayer ever a struggle for you? Does it ever feel as though it is more of a duty than a delight?

Have you attempted to pray and felt nothing at all? Are you doing your best to be close to God, yet it is as though He is a million miles away? Have you tried desperately to enter God's presence only to feel as though He was hiding from you?

I've been there. That's when I learned to pray when I felt nothing. That's when I learned to pray my way through a spiritual desert.

My Spiritual Desert

As a young Christian, I was knocked off stride the first time I went through a season of what I call "soul Sahara." When I surrendered my life to God, one of my greatest delights was enjoying a sense of His presence. But one day it was gone.

For days I trudged through this spiritual desert. Each day my soul became dustier and my heart emptier. God was gone, and I felt like I was going it alone. Scared that I had crossed some line with Him, I racked my brain trying to remember some serious sin I had committed or some devastating lie I had believed. But I got nothing. Confused, I was certain I had to be the only person to ever go through such a spiritually lonely season.

One day, one of my mature Christian friends asked me what was wrong. I told him.

"Oh, that happens to all of us," he responded. "When you are a new Christian, God's presence is all around and it seems like He answers every prayer 'Yes!' But one day, He withdraws the sense of His presence so that you learn to walk by faith, not feelings. He has not left you, even though it feels like it. He is just helping you grow up."

Then he looked me in the eye and said, "The issue is what you do now. You can press on or fall back. If you hang in there, eventually your awareness of God's presence will return."

After talking with my friend, I felt better. I did my best to press on in pursuing God by reading the Bible and praying. But I still felt as though I was praying into a big, black hole of nothingness.

Not long after that, I was reading Hebrews 11 and verse 6 caught my attention:

> *You can never please God without faith, without depending on him. Anyone who wants to come to God must believe that there is a God and that he rewards those who sincerely look for him.*
> HEBREWS 11:6 TLB

The first and the last phrase in that verse really caught my attention: "You can never please God without faith. . .he rewards those who sincerely look for him." So I decided to pursue God by faith and not feelings, trusting that He would eventually reward me by letting me "find" Him.

I went into the closet in my bedroom and closed the door. It was so dark in there that I could not see anything. I could not hear anything. I did not feel anything. Alone in the dark, I prayed a very bold prayer:

> *Okay, God. I can't see You. I can't hear You. I can't touch You. I can't smell You. I can't taste You. I can't feel You. I get it. You are hiding from me.*
> *I am going to pray anyway.*

I am praying by faith, not by feelings. I feel nothing. I am numb and dry inside. My soul is dark and barren. But You are worthy of my prayer. You are worthy of this block of time. So I am praying.

You promise to hear and answer prayer. You promise never to leave us or forsake us. You said that You reward those who diligently seek You. So here I am, by faith, diligently seeking You.

I opened my eyes and looked around. Still seeing and feeling nothing, I plunged ahead:

By faith, I bring You prayers of thanksgiving, adoration, confession, and supplication—whether I feel You here today or not. I am going to pray totally by faith. So here goes. God, I thank You because. . .

Before I could get the next words of praise out of my mouth, I felt it. It was the refreshing splash of a drop of God's presence on my barren, dry soul. As I continued praying, God's presence increased drop after drop until it was as though that closet were flooded. By the time I was done, it felt like a spiritual cloud-burst had drenched my soul. I was submerged in the replenishing water of the presence of God Himself. He had visited my closet and I knew it.

I wish I could say that it has always been that way when I tried to pray my way out of a dry time, but that is not the case. Often, I pray by faith and feel just as dry and parched as I did before I started. But I have learned that eventually my heavenly Father will say, "Enough." He will keep His promise and reward me with the treasure of Himself.

David's Desert

Near the end of his life, King David was chased off his throne, out of his city, and into the wilderness. His son Absalom had launched a vicious political and military overthrow and was chasing David with an army (2 Samuel 15–18). David found himself away from the temple, in the wilderness, running for his life, and struggling through deeply difficult days of spiritual dryness. This is what he prayed:

> You, God, are my God, earnestly I seek you; I thirst for you, my whole being longs for you, in a dry and parched land where there is no water.
> PSALM 63:1

In a place of deep distress and spiritual dryness, David decided to continue passionately pursuing God. He remembered God's powerful presence and glorious goodness in the past and praised the Lord by faith:

> I have seen you in the sanctuary and beheld your power and your glory. Because your love is better than life, my lips will glorify you. I will praise you as long as I live, and in your name I will lift up my hands.
> PSALM 63:2–4

As David desperately hung onto God, he realized that the Lord was hanging onto him and would help him through it all:

> Because you are my help, I sing in the shadow of your wings. I cling to you; your right hand upholds me.
> PSALM 63:7–8

Longing for Streams in the Desert

The psalmist was clearly in a spiritual desert when he wrote Psalm 42. He likened his spiritual thirst to the physical thirst of a deer that had run through a literal desert:

> As the deer pants for streams of water, so my soul pants for you, my God. My soul thirsts for God, for the living God. When can I go and meet with God? My tears have been my food day and night, while people say to me all day long, "Where is your God?"
> PSALM 42:1–3

David's way out of the dark desert? Choosing to pursue and praise God anyway:

> Why, my soul, are you downcast? Why so disturbed
> within me? Put your hope in God, for I will yet
> praise him, my Savior and my God.
> PSALM 42:5

"Why Have You Forsaken Me?"

When I am in a spiritual desert, it helps to remember that I am not alone and that I am in good company. I recall the sad words of Job as he sat in the dust scraping his wounds and counting his losses. I think of young Joseph chained in a cage on his way to Egypt. I picture him years later as a forgotten man in an Egyptian prison.

I consider Elijah, alone by the brook Cherith, and later isolated in wilderness wishing he were dead. I remember the apostle Paul, far from home, all alone, in the jail in Rome awaiting his execution.

I see Mary, the mother of Jesus, crying out to the Father to save her son and hearing nothing in return. And, of course, I remember Jesus, hanging on a cross, crying out, "My God, why have you forsaken me?"

Your Twenty–Eight Days to Powerful Prayer

There is only one good way to get through a spiritual desert: keep going until you come out on the other side. Persist in faith, expectation, praise, and prayer until the Sahara season is over and spiritual refreshment floods your soul again.

Questions to Consider

1. What encourages you about David's response to the spiritual dryness he described in Psalm 63?
2. Have you ever had a spiritually dry season? What got you through it?

3. What encouragement do you take in reading about biblical saints who had their own seasons when they couldn't "feel" God's presence?
4. Are you in a spiritually dry season now? What will you do to get through it?

DAY 28

PRAYER ISSUES

Praying When You Need a Miracle

Maybe you have made it this far through this book, and maybe you've applied what you've learned in your own life of prayer. Yet you are still facing an impossible situation. Are you being crushed by something outside your control? Do you feel helpless to do anything about it. . .and hopeless as a result?

Do you need a miracle?

If so, this is when you need to use the prayer for an impossible situation.

The Opportunity for a Miracle

This story begins nearly a decade after Jesus had been crucified and had risen from the dead. The first church had been born and was exploding in growth and influence. Herod Agrippa was king of Judea under Caesar's authority at the time, and to halt the threat of Jerusalem being overtaken by Christians, he had executed James, the brother of John. Then he imprisoned Peter and stationed sixteen soldiers to guard him in preparation for sentencing and execution the next day (Acts 12:1–4).

This was a hopelessly impossible situation for Peter. It would require more than a little luck. . .it would require a miracle.

That's where God came in.

Prayer advocate Armin Gesswein observed, "When God is about to do something great He starts with a difficulty. But when God is about to do something miraculous, He starts with an impossibility."[1]

I have studied every miracle in the Bible and have come to this conclusion: *There are no miracles without messes.* If it's not an impossible situation, we do not need God to do the impossible.

Peter was in a mess. He needed a miracle.

An Extraordinary Prayer

The church in Jerusalem had just witnessed the execution of one of its top leaders, and it looked like Peter would be next. These Christians needed a miracle, and they responded in the only way they could to such a hopeless situation—they prayed:

> *Peter was therefore kept in prison, but constant prayer was offered to God for him by the church.*
> ACTS 12:5 NKJV

Three important characteristics marked these people's prayers:

1. Their prayers were unceasing. The above verse says that the people offered "constant prayer." They didn't send up short, concise little prayers and then go on about their business. No, they kept praying all night until God gave them an answer.

These people understood something we need to grasp today: impossible situations demand extraordinary prayers. Could it be that we do not see more major answers to prayer because we stop too soon and quit too easily? Instead of doing that, we should follow the example of those early Christians in Jerusalem.

2. Their prayers were united. The Bible states that it was "the church" that prayed for Peter's deliverance. Acts 12:12 says that "many people had gathered and were praying."

As you read in Day 19, Jesus promised that the unity of two or three in prayer produces answered prayer (Matthew 18:19–20). Praying on your own is good and essential for your spiritual growth, but often miracles come as a result of united prayer.

3. Their prayers were urgent. The situation was urgent, and urgent situations demand urgent prayers, desperate situations demand desperate prayers, and extraordinary needs demand extraordinary prayers.

An Extraordinary Answer

In response to the church's extraordinary prayers, God gave an extraordinary answer, sending an angel to rescue Peter. The angel arrived at the heavily guarded prison, made the chains fall off Peter's wrists, and then escorted him out of the cell without disturbing the guards:

> The night before Herod was to bring him to trial, Peter was sleeping between two soldiers, bound with two chains, and sentries stood guard at the entrance. Suddenly an angel of the Lord appeared and a light shone in the cell. He struck Peter on the side and woke him up. "Quick, get up!" he said, and the chains fell off Peter's wrists. Then the angel said to him, "Put on your clothes and sandals." And Peter did so. "Wrap your cloak around you and follow me," the angel told him.
> Acts 12:6–8

Note that Peter was "sleeping between two soldiers and bound with two chains" (Acts 12:6). Why was he asleep? Could it be because he was right with God and ready to face death? Was it because he had remembered Jesus telling him that he would reach old age (John 21:18)? Or perhaps it was because he knew people were praying for him.

Anyway, back to the story:

> Peter followed him out of the prison, but he had no idea that what the angel was doing was really happening; he thought he was seeing a vision. They passed the first and second guards and came to the iron gate leading to the city. It opened for them by itself, and they went through it. When they had walked the length of one street, suddenly the angel left him. Then Peter came to himself and said, "Now I know without a doubt

*that the Lord sent his angel and rescued me from Herod's
clutches and from everything the Jewish people were
hoping would happen."*
ACTS 12:9–11

The angel made it possible for Peter to pass by the guards
undetected and also opened a huge gate so the apostle could
escape. The church's urgent, united, unceasing prayers had been
answered. God had provided a miracle. Peter was saved!

The Prayers of Ordinary People

When Peter finally realized the reality of what God had just
done for him, he headed to the home of a woman named Mary,
who was the mother of John Mark, the writer of the Gospel of
Mark. A large crowd of people were gathered there, still praying
(Acts 12:12).

What happened next is both a little humorous and also a big
reminder of the kind of people God often uses as prayer warriors:

> *Peter knocked at the outer entrance, and a servant named
> Rhoda came to answer the door. When she recognized Peter's
> voice, she was so overjoyed she ran back without opening it
> and exclaimed, "Peter is at the door!"*
> ACTS 12:13–14

In Rhoda's excitement that Peter had been freed, the servant girl
left him standing *outside* the unopened door and then ran back
to tell the people that Peter was at the door. Their response?
"You're out of your mind" (Acts 12:15).

Imagine that! These people had been praying for Peter's
release, but when God miraculously answered, they left Peter
standing at their door! Not only that, they told the young woman
who announced that Peter was free that she was crazy! This tells
me that while their prayers were unceasing, united, and urgent,
they lacked confident faith—like many of our prayers today.

I take comfort in the fact that while these people offered

extraordinary prayer, they were just ordinary Christians. They weren't super saints; they were people just like you and me. They were just ordinary people who hoped in the power of prayer:

> *When she kept insisting that it was so, they said, "It must be his angel." But Peter kept on knocking, and when they opened the door and saw him, they were astonished. Peter motioned with his hand for them to be quiet and described how the Lord had brought him out of prison.*
> ACTS 12:15–17

I cannot fully explain or understand why, but God often chooses to remain inactive until we activate Him in prayer. If the church had not prayed so fervently, would Peter have been rescued? I doubt it. Otherwise God would not have told us the story about this extraordinary prayer meeting.

The Power of Unceasing, United, Urgent Prayer Today

It was Wednesday afternoon. Doug had just left his daughter Grace's bedside in the ICU. She had brain cancer and faced soon and certain death without a very risky operation. The doctor had told Doug that the odds of her even surviving the operation were slim. And even if she survived surgery, the doctor said, the lethal cancer would probably return. But the surgery was her only hope.

Scared and desperate, Doug went to the hospital gift shop looking for comfort and hope. He found a little book on prayer, bought it, and then went to the lobby and started reading. He drank in the story of Elijah asking for a miracle and God sending fire from heaven. He devoured the story of the two blind men asking Jesus for healing and then having their sight fully restored. He read about a desperate mother asking Jesus to heal her daughter and the girl receiving deliverance immediately.

Inspired, he called his church and told some people that he believed that if they would pray in unity and urgency, God would do a miracle for Grace. They took the call to pray seriously. They also contacted other churches in their area and asked them to do the same. That night, hundreds of people joined together with Doug in unceasing, urgent prayer for Grace's healing.

The next day Doug sat in the waiting room as the operation went on and on. Finally, the doctor emerged, smiling. "I have good news, Doug," the doctor said. "Despite the odds, Grace survived the surgery. On top of that, we were able to get all the cancer. She is in post-op now and is doing great!"

Doug had received the first part of the miracle he had prayed for.

Nine months later, Doug sent me an email:

> Grace just returned from her exam. The doctor gave her a clean bill of health. The cancer has not returned. The doctor said that if it had not returned by now, it wouldn't.
> Do you know what this means?
> God fully healed my daughter!
> We got all the miracle we prayed for!

Your Twenty-Eight Days to Powerful Prayer

We do not always need united, unceasing, urgent prayer for a miracle. But when we do, we can thank the Lord that miracles are possible. Turn your impossible situation into a call to extraordinary prayer. See what God can do.

Questions to Consider

1. What about Peter's story caught your attention?
2. What did you like about what happened with Doug and his daughter Grace?
3. What is your overwhelming need and/or impossible situation right now?
4. How can you get others to join you in united, unceasing, urgent prayer for the necessary breakthrough?

Notes

1. Armin Gesswein, www.beliefnet.com/quotes/christian/a/
   armin-gesswein/when-god-is-about-to-do-something-
   great-he-starts.aspx (accessed February 12, 2019)

Final Thoughts

Congratulations! You have completed *28 Days to Powerful Prayer*.

At this point in the journey, you have studied the privilege and power of prayer. You have created a plan for your daily prayer time. You have learned and are applying the seven primary types of prayer. And you have removed the obstacles to answered prayer and put into place significant boosters to your prayer life.

Beyond all of that, you have wrestled through some of the most important issues of prayer, including how to pray the scriptures, how to fast, how to pray for your spiritual leaders, and how to pray biblically for others. You have even learned what to do when you are in a spiritual desert or when you need a miracle.

You have built a strong foundation in prayer and hopefully you have seen answers beginning to come. But the goal is not merely to enjoy a powerful month of prayer but to develop a powerful *life* of prayer.

Let me offer a few suggestions for building on the foundation we've already laid:

1. We're told that it takes three to four weeks to develop a habit and an additional three to four weeks to develop a lifestyle. Therefore, review this book this month, a chapter each day. Tone up your prayer life in the areas of prayer discussed in each chapter. You will be surprised what you missed the first time through!

2. Ask someone to join you as a prayer partner. Read and pray through this book together. It will amaze you what you learn by helping teach another person.

3. Pick a few of the chapters and focus on them this month, seeking to master the aspect of prayer they discuss.

4. Read and pray through another spiritually challenging book this month.[1]

One More Thought

Please do not assume that I consider this book to be the ultimate word for your prayer life. No—God is infinite, and prayer has vast untapped opportunities. May this book merely be the launching pad for so much more!

Notes

1. If you enjoy my writing style, you might consider reading my other books:
   - *28 Days to Knowing God* (Uhrichsville, Ohio: Barbour Publishing, 2019)
   - *The 21 Most Effective Prayers in the Bible* (Uhrichsville, Ohio: Barbour Publishing, 2005)
   - *Prayer: Timeless Secret of High Impact Leaders* (Chattanooga, Tennessee: AMG Publishers, 2008)
   - *Praying for Your Children*, with Elmer Towns (Shippensburg, Pennsylvania: Destiny Image, 2011)
   - *Praying for Your Job*, with Elmer Towns (Shippensburg, Pennsylvania: Destiny Image, 2011)

Suggestions for Using This Book

1. Small Groups: *28 Days to Powerful Prayer* is a great resource for small group study. Every chapter includes several scriptures to discuss and several challenging application questions. Depending on your group, you could use it several ways:

- Study two chapters a week for fourteen weeks.
- Study four chapters a week for seven weeks.
- Study seven chapters a week for four weeks.

For the group I lead, I am planning to use the "four chapters a week for seven weeks" plan.

2. Pastors and Churches: Many churches like to start campaigns to stimulate spiritual growth in the lives of their people. *28 Days to Powerful Prayer* is an excellent tool to use as part of a church prayer campaign. Your church could use this book as a text for your weekly prayer meeting or, as we mentioned above, as a good tool for small groups and Sunday school classes.

Also from Dave Earley

28 Days to Knowing God

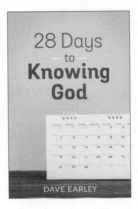

Want to know God? Use His Word as your guide! This easy-to-read volume studies major names and characteristics of God as found in the Bible, speaking both to believers and seekers—people of all ages, backgrounds, and maturity levels—with an uplifting message: God is awesome, and you can know Him.

Paperback / 978-1-64352-004-9 / $9.99